THE GREAT AUSSIE ROAST

Smith Street Books

Published in 2023 by Smith Street Books
Naarm (Melbourne) | Australia
smithstreetbooks.com

ISBN: 978-1-9227-5480-6

All rights reserved. No part of this book may be reproduced or transmitted by any person or entity, in any form or by any means, electronic or mechanical, including photocopying, recording, scanning or by any storage and retrieval system, without the prior written permission of the publishers and copyright holders.

Smith Street Books respectfully acknowledges the Wurundjeri People of the Kulin Nation, who are the Traditional Owners of the land on which we work, and we pay our respects to their Elders past and present.

Please note that the recipes in this book have previously appeared in *Roast*, published by Smith Street Books in 2017.

Copyright recipes, text & design © Smith Street Books
Copyright photography © Chris Middleton

Publisher: Paul McNally
Project manager: Aisling Coughlan
Editor: Katri Hilden
Proofreader: Ariana Klepac
Recipe development: Aisling Coughlan, Lucy Heaver & Caroline Griffiths
Introduction text: Jane Price
Design concept: Murray Batten
Design layout: Heather Menzies, Studio31 Graphics
Photographer: Chris Middleton
Art director & Stylist: Stephanie Stamatis
Food preparation: Caroline Griffiths & Aisling Coughlan

Printed & bound in China by C&C Offset Printing Co., Ltd.

Book 270
10 9 8 7 6 5 4 3 2 1

THE GREAT AUSSIE ROAST

NEW CLASSICS
& OLD FAVOURITES

louise franc

INTRODUCTION 6

01 VEGETABLES 10

02 FISH & SHELLFISH 30

03 POULTRY 52

04 MEAT 84

05 SIDES 116

06 DESSERTS 152

INDEX 174

INTRODUCTION

The roast dinner is a much-loved staple in many Australian homes. It can be an occasion, a get-together, or simply a comfort when nothing else will do. The fact that Australia has become a wonderful collection of so many cultures means that today's roasts are no longer just a straightforward roasted meat and veg affair, instead we can enjoy the very best spices and flavours from around the world – a celebratory meal that celebrates us all.

The roast dinner would seem to be embedded in our psyche as a symbol of happiness and security. Perhaps it's a lingering subliminal memory from our early days, when a successful hunt meant a fire, a spit and roasted meat carved up ceremoniously by the leader, with a special piece for everyone, often according to social hierarchy. Today's roast doesn't always involve carving; it often doesn't even involve meat; and it is rarely – if ever – portioned out according to social status. But the ritual of cooking a complete meal in one tray and taking it to the table to share out and enjoy with others, continues to create an atmosphere of ceremony, warmth and festivity.

Some of the recipes in this book are celebratory and perfect for an 'occasion', but most are just as suitable for a weeknight dinner. While the cooking time might be a little longer than other dishes, the preparation of any roast dish is generally easy and fuss-free. Once a roast is in the oven, you can walk away and do something else while the meat bakes to tenderness and the vegetables caramelise to soft sweetness with a golden crunch. There is little washing up, and sometimes there are even leftovers for another meal.

The only criteria for these old classic and new favourite roast recipes is that they should be cooked in the oven and taste wonderful. Today, when so many of us have so little time, yet are conscious that sharing a healthy family dinner of unprocessed fresh food is beneficial to health and wellbeing, the no-fuss, simply delicious oven roast is making a huge comeback.

EQUIPMENT

ROASTING TINS: There is truly very little equipment required for oven roasting – which only adds to the appeal and makes washing up pretty easy. One or two deep roasting tins will do the trick – a large one for cooking a whole bird or large joint of meat with veggies, and a smaller one. A good-quality tin with a heavy base will distribute and hold the heat better, and prevent your dish from burning. Beware of roasting tins with fold-away handles – the handles are tricky to fold out again when they are hot, especially when wearing oven gloves. Your tin should be a maximum of 8 cm deep – deep enough to hold liquid safely, but not so deep that it prevents the air circulating around its contents. It should also be large enough to hold your ingredients in one layer; otherwise your food will steam rather than roast.

If you are concerned about fat, you can put your meat or poultry on a rack in the tin, to hold it up above the drippings. This can be useful if you're roasting pork or duck – fattier meats that produce more juices.

CASSEROLE DISHES: For dishes that need to be covered, a casserole dish with a tight-fitting lid is perfect. A recipe will often stipulate a 'flameproof casserole dish', or sometimes an 'ovenproof frying pan'. This is because the recipe requires ingredients to be browned on the stovetop first and then transferred to the oven. Your dish needs to be tough enough to withstand direct heat to its base; or your frying pan needs to be free of any plastic elements, such as handles that might melt in the oven. If you own neither of these, you can use a frying pan to brown ingredients on the stovetop, then transfer to your casserole dish and place in the oven. It just means dirtying two pots.

THERMOMETER: Many cooks use a meat thermometer – you can pick one up from any kitchenware shop or even some supermarkets. If you have any worries about the accuracy of your oven, an instant-read thermometer will let you know how your meat is doing. Poke the thermometer 5 cm into the middle of the roast, being careful not to let it touch the bone.

YOUR OVEN: The majority of modern ovens are fan-forced, and these are the temperatures given in the recipes that follow. If you don't have a fan-forced oven, you will need to set the temperature higher than that given, usually around 20°C.

Every oven is different though and, especially if yours is older, you will need to get used to its particular foibles.

You will notice that many pieces of meat or poultry in this book are cooked at a high temperature for a short amount of time, before the oven temperature is reduced; this is to brown and seal the meat before slowly cooking it through.

EXTRAS: It is handy to keep some unwaxed kitchen string in your drawer for trussing meat or chicken. A pair of sharp kitchen scissors or poultry shears are also useful for jointing birds.

ROASTING MEAT

CUTS OF MEAT: Traditional roasts use the tender meat cuts, such as tenderloin, fillet or ribs, while the tougher cuts usually need longer, slower cooking, often in liquid, to tenderise them. Both types of dish are included in this book: for example, the mini lamb roasts on page 104, and the slow-cooked beef pot roast, made with chuck or blade, on page 108, or the pork knuckle on page 92. Slow-braising in liquid is a great way to tenderise cheaper cuts of meat, which are often full of flavour.

If your meat has the bone still, it will take longer to cook than a boneless piece. A boneless cut will often be rolled and trussed to hold it together and make it a similar thickness throughout for even cooking.

PREPARING THE MEAT: Take your meat out of the fridge about 30 minutes before roasting, so that it comes to room temperature for even cooking. If browning the meat on the stovetop before placing it in the oven, season the meat after you've seared it, as adding salt before you brown it can draw out too much moisture. You might also be instructed to baste the meat during cooking – this simply means spoon some of the pan juices over the meat to keep it moist.

COOKING TIMES: These are given in each recipe but, as a rough guide, below are some cooking times per uncooked weight:

- Beef: for rare, 20–25 minutes per 500 g. For medium, 30 minutes per 500 g.
- Lamb: for rare, 20–25 minutes per 500 g. For medium, 25–30 minutes per 500 g.
- Pork: 30 minutes per 500 g.

REST BEFORE CARVING: When you take roasted meat out of the oven, it is important to let it rest before you carve. Resting cooked meat for around 15 minutes allows it to reabsorb all its juices. If you carve too quickly, the juices will run out all over your carving board and the meat will be dry and tough. Cover the meat loosely with foil (not tightly, or it will steam and overcook under the foil) and leave in a warm place. If you like, you can use this time to make the gravy. Just like basting, resting the meat is all about keeping it as juicy as possible.

To carve, place a damp cloth under your board to ensure that it doesn't move around. Use a carving fork to hold the rested roast in place, and slice across the grain of the meat at a consistent angle with a very sharp carving knife. Stack the slices of meat on a warmed plate as you carve, so that they retain their juices and don't go cold.

ROASTING VEGETABLES AROUND THE MEAT: Meat will usually take longer to cook than vegetables. So get the meat in first, then prepare the vegetables to go around it. They need to be cut into similar-sized pieces so they cook at the same rate. Always use a large enough roasting tin so that your vegetables are not crammed together, causing them to steam rather than crisp up.

Vegetables that roast well include:

Potatoes (an all-rounder variety, such as desiree or sebago), sweet potato, pumpkin, turnip, parsnip, whole carrots, beetroot and onions. These all need around 1 hour in the oven.
Fennel – a large bulb cut into quarters should take 30–45 minutes in the oven.

Cooking a great roast is all about timing. Everything needs to come together at the same time: meat, veggies, gravy and side dishes. When you are working out your vegetable cooking times, don't forget you will rest the meat for 15–20 minutes before serving, and that your vegetables can finish off cooking during this time. So if your roast needs 2 hours in the oven and your potatoes and onions need 1 hour, add them to the roasting tin when the meat has been cooking for 1 hour 20 minutes. Once the meat has been removed from the tin, you can turn up the oven for the last minutes of the cooking time so that the potatoes get a good crisp finish. If you are making gravy, move the vegetables to a new baking tray and pop them back in the oven to crisp up while you use the roasting tin to make the gravy.

MAKING GRAVY: For traditional gravy, spoon off all but 2 tablespoons of the meat juices from the roasting tin. Put the roasting tin on the stovetop over low heat and stir about 1 tablespoon of plain flour into the pan juices. Stir with a wooden spoon over the heat for a couple of minutes to 'cook' the flour, scraping up all the bits from the bottom of the roasting tin. Then start to stir in stock, water or vegetable cooking water, a cupful at a time, stirring well until the liquid is absorbed and there are no lumps. You will need around 4 cupfuls of liquid, depending on how thick or thin you like your gravy. Once you have added all the liquid, simmer the gravy, stirring occasionally, for 8–10 minutes until reduced and thickened.

ROASTING POULTRY

GOLDEN RULES FOR POULTRY: Raw or undercooked poultry can be a potential cause of food poisoning if it is treated carelessly. If you are using frozen chicken, always thaw it thoroughly in the fridge, rather than leaving it out at room temperature. And once it is thawed, use it within 24 hours. When you have prepared raw poultry, always wash the chopping board, knives and other utensils thoroughly in hot soapy water. Don't ever carve the cooked chicken on the unwashed board where you handled it raw.

TRUSSING: If a chicken isn't stuffed, then it should be trussed for roasting; otherwise the breast cavity gapes open and hot air can circulate inside, causing the breasts to cook faster than the legs and wings, which can make the breast meat dry out. Trussing simply means tying the legs together with unwaxed kitchen string to keep the cavity closed. Rinse inside the cavity before trussing, and tuck the wing tips under the bird at the same time.

STUFFING: Flavours such lemon, garlic, onion, sage, thyme and other herbs are often used to stuff the bird. A traditional bread stuffing absorbs some of the delicious juices of the meat, while also infusing the bird with the flavourings. If you don't want to serve stuffing with your roast, then simply put your flavourings of choice such as herbs, sliced lemon or onion inside the cavity before trussing.

An alternative to stuffing the bird is to loosen the skin over the breasts by sliding your finger under the skin and running it up and down to detach it from the flesh. You can then spread some flavoured butter into the gap between the skin and breasts.

TESTING YOUR BIRD: Overcooking poultry will cause it to dry out, but undercooked poultry can be dangerous. There are many different methods for cooking chicken and turkey – some cooks prefer faster cooking at a higher temperature; others, the opposite – but as a rough guide, a stuffed chicken needs about 30 minutes per 500 g in a 180°C fan-forced oven. Whatever cooking method you use, to test if your roast bird is ready, insert a skewer into the thickest part of the thigh. When the juices run clear with no sign of pink, it is cooked through. Remove from the oven, cover the bird loosely with foil and leave to rest for around 15 minutes before carving. As with other meats, resting the bird lets the juices reabsorb into the meat. Some people leave it to rest upside down so that the juices all run into the breast meat, which can be a little drier.

01

VEGETABLES

ROAST PORTOBELLO MUSHROOMS
WITH BLUE CHEESE & PINE NUT STUFFING

p.12

ROASTED EGGPLANT WITH
TAHINI SAUCE & POMEGRANATE

p.15

MUSHROOM & WINTER
VEGETABLE WELLINGTON

p.16

ROASTED ROOT VEGIES

p.20

COUSCOUS-STUFFED CAPSICUM

p.23

WHOLE STUFFED PUMPKIN

p.24

HARISSA-ROASTED CAULIFLOWER
WITH FIG & YOGHURT SAUCE

p.27

ROASTED GARLIC & TOMATO TART

p.28

ROAST PORTOBELLO MUSHROOMS WITH BLUE CHEESE & PINE NUT STUFFING

Serves 4

- 8 medium-sized portobello mushrooms
- 40 g butter
- 2 French shallots, finely diced
- 2 garlic cloves, crushed
- 1 generous teaspoon picked thyme leaves
- 80 g (1 cup) fresh breadcrumbs
- 200 g stilton, crumbled
- 40 g (¼ cup) pine nuts, toasted
- 1 tablespoon olive oil
- baby red sorrel leaves, to garnish (optional)

CHARRED RED CAPSICUM SAUCE

- 2 red capsicums
- 150 g sour cream
- 1 teaspoon lemon juice
- 1 garlic clove, crushed

— To char the capsicums for the sauce, place them on a heated barbecue, or directly on a gas burner over medium heat, and cook for 7–10 minutes, rotating regularly with tongs, until blackened all over. Transfer to a zip-lock bag and place in the freezer. Once cooled, gently remove the skin, stems and seeds.

— Place the capsicum flesh into the bowl of a small food processor, along with the sour cream, lemon juice and garlic. Blend until combined into a smooth sauce. Set aside.

— Preheat the oven to 170°C (fan-forced). Line a baking tray with baking paper.

— Remove the stalks from the mushrooms. Trim and discard the woody ends, then finely chop the stalks.

— Melt the butter in a frying pan over medium heat and sauté the shallot, garlic and chopped mushroom stalks for 5–7 minutes, or until softened. Stir the thyme through, transfer to a bowl and leave to cool slightly.

— Add the breadcrumbs, stilton and pine nuts to the shallot mixture and mix to combine.

— Brush the outside of the mushrooms with the olive oil. Divide the stuffing between the mushrooms, patting it down firmly to keep it in place.

— Transfer the stuffed mushrooms to the baking tray and roast for 15 minutes.

— Serve warm, with the roasted capsicum sauce, garnished with baby red sorrel leaves if desired.

ROASTED EGGPLANT WITH TAHINI SAUCE & POMEGRANATE

Serves 4

— Using a sharp knife, cut each eggplant in half lengthways, then score the cut side of each half in a diamond pattern. Season generously with salt, and leave to sit for 30 minutes.

— Meanwhile, grind the cumin seeds using a mortar and pestle, mix with the olive oil and set aside.

— Preheat the oven to 180°C (fan-forced).

— Rinse the salted eggplant thoroughly with water, then pat dry with paper towel. Brush each cut side with the cumin and oil mixture, then place on a baking tray, cut side up.

— Transfer to the oven and roast for 20 minutes, or until the flesh is tender.

— While the eggplant is roasting, combine all the tahini sauce ingredients in a small bowl, mixing well. Season to taste with salt and freshly ground black pepper and set aside.

— To remove the seeds from the pomegranate, cut the pomegranate in half. Hold one half, cut side down, in the palm of your hand with your fingers spread, over a wide bowl. Use the back of a ladle or a rolling pin to firmly tap the skin of the pomegranate — the seeds should fall out into the bowl. Once it looks like all the seeds have been released, pick through the bowl to remove any white bits of the pith that have fallen in.

— Place the roasted eggplant on a platter and drizzle evenly with the tahini sauce. Scatter over the parsley and pomegranate seeds and serve.

4 medium-sized eggplants

1 teaspoon cumin seeds

2 tablespoons olive oil

1 pomegranate

2 tablespoons chopped parsley

TAHINI SAUCE

1 tablespoon tahini

250 g (1 cup) Greek-style yoghurt

1 garlic clove, crushed

½ teaspoon pomegranate molasses

zest and juice of ½ lemon

MUSHROOM & WINTER VEGETABLE WELLINGTON

Serves 6–8

— Place the dried porcini in a small bowl, cover with 125 ml (½ cup) hot water and set aside to soak.

— Melt the butter in a large saucepan over medium heat and add the onion, garlic, celery, carrot and leek. Give everything a good stir until the vegetables are well coated in the butter, then stir through the thyme. Season well with salt and freshly ground black pepper.

— Reduce the heat to medium–low, partially cover with a lid and cook, stirring occasionally, for about 20 minutes, or until the vegetables are completely soft. Stir the chestnuts through, check and adjust the seasoning if necessary, then set aside to cool.

— Preheat the oven to 180°C (fan-forced). Line a large baking tray with foil.

— Blitz the fresh mushrooms in a food processor and set aside. Strain the porcini mushrooms, reserving the liquid, and finely chop.

— Heat the olive oil in a large frying pan over medium heat and add the porcini and sage. Cook for 2–3 minutes, stirring regularly, then increase the heat to medium–high. Add the chopped fresh mushrooms, season well and cook, stirring frequently, until the mixture has reduced and is starting to brown.

— Deglaze the pan with the sherry, stirring until the liquid is absorbed. Pour in the reserved porcini soaking liquid and reduce the heat to medium. Cook, stirring frequently, until the liquid is completely absorbed.

— Transfer the mushroom mixture to a large bowl. Add the sautéed vegetables, then stir through the breadcrumbs, lemon zest and parsley. Check the seasoning and adjust if necessary.

— Steam the kale for 3–4 minutes, or until wilted. Drain well and set aside.

- 20 g dried porcini mushrooms
- 30 g butter
- 1 onion, finely chopped
- 3 garlic cloves, finely chopped
- 1 celery stalk, finely diced
- 1 carrot, finely diced
- 1 leek, white part only, sliced
- 2 teaspoons chopped thyme
- 100 g chestnuts, finely chopped; tinned or vacuum-packed are fine
- 300 g mixed fresh mushrooms, such as field, cup and shiitake, roughly chopped
- 1 tablespoon olive oil
- 8 sage leaves, chopped
- 2 tablespoons Pedro Ximénez, or any good-quality sweet Spanish sherry
- 70 g fresh breadcrumbs
- zest of 1 lemon
- large handful chopped parsley
- 300 g kale, coarse stems removed, leaves chopped
- plain flour, for dusting
- 350 g block of frozen puff pastry, thawed
- 100 g stilton
- 1 free-range egg, whisked with 1 tablespoon milk

— On a lightly floured work surface, roll out the puff pastry to a large rectangle, about 5 mm thick. Squeeze as much liquid as possible from the steamed kale and scatter it over the pastry, leaving a 2 cm border around the edges. Spoon the vegetable mixture onto the long side of the pastry nearest to you, then form into a large log — it will look huge! Break the stilton into small chunks and dot over the vegetables.

— Brush the edges of the pastry with the egg wash, then gently lift the side that's nearest to you and roll the pastry into a large sausage roll — the two long edges should overlap by about 4 cm.

— Transfer to the lined baking tray, seam side down, and close the short ends of the wellington by pinching and pleating the pastry.

— Brush the pastry with the egg wash, then cut some slits in the top using a sharp knife, to let the steam escape.

— Bake for 30–40 minutes, or until the pastry is browned and crisp. Remove from the oven and let the pastry settle for a minute or two before carving.

— While the wellington is still in the oven, make the mushroom gravy. Melt the butter in a saucepan over medium heat. Add the mushrooms, shallot and thyme, increase the heat to medium-high and cook, stirring frequently, for about 8 minutes, or until slightly browned. Add the flour and cook, stirring, for 2–3 minutes, or until the flour looks lightly toasted. Add the stock 250 ml (1 cup) at a time, stirring constantly until the sauce has thickened after each addition. Add the soy sauce and season with salt and freshly ground black pepper. Cook for a further minute.

— Cut the wellington into thick slices and serve with the mushroom gravy poured over the top.

MUSHROOM GRAVY

50 g butter

250 g mushrooms, such as field and cup mushrooms, finely sliced

4 French shallots, finely chopped

4 thyme sprigs

35 g (¼ cup) plain flour

750 ml (3 cups) vegetable stock

1 tablespoon soy sauce

Mushroom & winter vegetable wellington

ROASTED ROOT VEGIES

Serves 6

— To make the berbere spice mix, toast the whole spices lightly in a dry frying pan over medium heat until fragrant. Using a mortar and pestle, grind to a fine powder with all the remaining spice mix ingredients. Reserve 2 tablespoons of the berbere spice mix for the chickpeas; any left-over spice mix can be stored in a small airtight container and used in other dishes.

— Add the tahini sauce ingredients to a small screw-top jar. Pour in 60 ml (¼ cup) water, seal the lid on and shake until well combined. If you would like a thinner sauce, add a little more water. Set aside.

— Preheat the oven to 200°C (fan-forced).

— Combine the rosemary, thyme and olive oil in a small screw-top jar and season well with salt and freshly ground black pepper.

— Place the beetroot in a small roasting tin and drizzle with1 tablespoon of the herbed oil mixture. Mix well with your hands, then roast for 50 minutes.

— Place the carrots, parsnip, celeriac and sweet potato in a large roasting tin and pour over half of the remaining oil. Rub the vegetables in the oil, then transfer to the oven and roast for 20 minutes.

— Add the pumpkin and remaining herbed oil to the roasting tin, stirring to combine, then roast for a further 20 minutes, or until all the vegetables are cooked through.

— Meanwhile, melt the butter in a frying pan over medium heat. Add the garlic and cook, stirring, until just starting to brown. Add the chickpeas and increase the heat to medium–high. Add 2 tablespoons of the reserved berbere spice mix and cook, stirring constantly, for 4–5 minutes, or until the chickpeas are dry and starting to become crisp. Set aside.

— Pile the roasted vegetables onto a serving platter and scatter with the spiced chickpeas. Drizzle with the tahini sauce, scatter with the cashews and parsley, sprinkle with the sumac and serve.

2 rosemary sprigs, leaves picked
small handful thyme, leaves picked
90 ml olive oil
2 large beetroot, peeled and cut into chunks
6 baby carrots, scrubbed
3 parsnips, peeled and cut in half
250 g celeriac, peeled and cut into chunks
1 sweet potato, cut into chunks
250 g pumpkin, peeled and cut into chunks
20 g butter
1 garlic clove, finely chopped
2 x 420 g tins chickpeas, drained
40 g (¼ cup) cashews, chopped
small handful parsley, roughly chopped
1 tablespoon sumac

BERBERE SPICE MIX

1 teaspoon cumin seeds
4 whole cloves
3 cardamom pods
½ teaspoon black peppercorns
1 teaspoon fenugreek seeds
1 teaspoon coriander seeds
4 small dried red chillies
1 teaspoon salt
½ teaspoon ground ginger
½ teaspoon ground turmeric
2 tablespoons smoked paprika
¼ teaspoon ground allspice
pinch of ground cinnamon

TAHINI SAUCE

3 tablespoons tahini
juice of 1½ lemons
1 garlic clove, finely chopped
1 teaspoon salt

COUSCOUS-STUFFED CAPSICUM

Serves 4

- 4 red or yellow capsicums
- 185 g (1 cup) couscous
- 375 ml (1½ cups) hot vegetable stock
- 60 ml (¼ cup) olive oil
- 4 French shallots, finely chopped
- 3 garlic cloves, finely chopped
- 2 teaspoons ground cumin
- zest of 2 lemons
- large handful parsley, roughly chopped
- 60 g (½ cup) slivered almonds, toasted
- 2 tablespoons currants
- 100 g (⅔ cup) crumbled feta
- juice of 1 lemon

— Preheat the oven to 160°C (fan-forced).

— Using a sharp knife, slice the tops off the capsicums, then scoop out the seeds and white membrane. Blanch the capsicums in a large saucepan of boiling water for 5 minutes. Drain, then transfer to a plate, placing the capsicums upside down to drain completely.

— Tip the couscous into a shallow bowl and pour the hot stock over. Leave to stand for 5 minutes, then fluff up the grains with a fork.

— Heat 1 tablespoon of the olive oil in a frying pan over medium heat. Add the shallot and garlic and cook for about 10 minutes, or until light golden. Stir in the cumin and cook for a further 2 minutes. Add the lemon zest and parsley and stir well to combine. Remove from the heat and set aside.

— Drizzle 1 tablespoon of the remaining olive oil over the couscous and season with salt and freshly ground black pepper. Add the shallot mixture, slivered almonds, currants, feta and lemon juice and stir well to combine.

— Fill the hollow capsicums with the couscous mixture, then sit them upright in a baking dish. Drizzle with the remaining oil.

— Transfer to the oven and roast for about 30 minutes, or until the couscous is lightly browned on top. Enjoy warm.

WHOLE STUFFED PUMPKIN

Serves 8

60 ml (¼ cup) olive oil
200 g uncracked freekeh, rinsed
1½ teaspoons coriander seeds, crushed
1½ teaspoons cumin seeds, crushed
1 litre (4 cups) vegetable stock
40 g (⅓ cup) slivered almonds, toasted
3 large garlic cloves, finely chopped
70 g (½ cup) dried cranberries
2 large rosemary sprigs, leaves picked and chopped
large handful parsley, roughly chopped
1 large pumpkin, weighing at least 2 kg
60 ml (¼ cup) maple syrup
60 ml (¼ cup) apple cider vinegar

— Heat a small splash of the olive oil in a saucepan over medium heat. Add the freekeh and coriander and cumin seeds and cook until the mixture starts to sizzle and pop. Add the stock and simmer, stirring occasionally, for 45 minutes, or up to 1 hour, until the freekeh is cooked through. Transfer to a large bowl and add the almonds, garlic, cranberries, rosemary and parsley. Mix well and season to taste.

— Meanwhile, preheat the oven to 200°C (fan-forced).

— Using a large kitchen knife, cut out the top of the pumpkin and set aside as a lid. Scoop out the seeds and fibres with a spoon and discard. If your pumpkin is very thick in places, scoop out a little of the pumpkin until it is even on all sides — this will help the pumpkin to cook evenly.

— In a small bowl, combine the maple syrup, vinegar and remaining olive oil. Season with salt and freshly ground black pepper, then pour over the freekeh. Toss to combine and check the seasoning.

— Spoon the freekeh into the pumpkin shell. Place the pumpkin lid on top and wrap the whole pumpkin in two layers of foil.

— Place on a baking tray, transfer to the oven and roast for 1 hour. Remove the foil and roast for at least another 1 hour. The pumpkin may seem soft at this stage when tested with a sharp knife, but it takes a long time to cook all the way through. You can test it's done by inserting a knife into the middle and scraping off a little of the pumpkin flesh inside. If it is still a little fibrous, cook the pumpkin for longer.

— Allow the pumpkin to rest for 10 minutes before slicing into large wedges and serving.

HARISSA-ROASTED CAULIFLOWER WITH FIG & YOGHURT SAUCE

Serves 4

— Preheat the oven to 160°C (fan-forced). Line a deep-sided baking dish with foil.

— To make the harissa, cut two of the chillies in half lengthways and remove the seeds and membranes. Roughly chop all four chillies and set aside.

— In a small frying pan, toast the caraway, coriander and cumin seeds over medium heat for a minute or two, until fragrant. Tip the toasted seeds into the small bowl of a food processor. Add the remaining harissa ingredients, including the chopped chillies, and blend until everything is chopped and has transformed into a thickish paste.

— Mix half the harissa through the 185 g (¾ cup) yoghurt, then taste to check if it is spicy or hot enough for you. You can add more harissa, until the heat is to your liking.

— Remove the core and any outer leaves from the cauliflower. Brush the harissa yoghurt mixture all over the cauliflower, ensuring it is evenly coated on all sides.

— Transfer the coated cauliflower to the baking dish and into the oven. Roast for 30 minutes.

— Add 125 ml (½ cup) water to the dish, cover with a lid or foil, and roast the cauliflower for a further 20 minutes, or until tender.

— Meanwhile, in a small bowl, mix together the fig and yoghurt sauce ingredients until well combined.

— Serve the cauliflower warm, with the fig and yoghurt sauce, sprinkled with the almonds and parsley.

- 185 g (¾ cup) plain yoghurt
- 1 whole cauliflower
- 25 g (¼ cup) flaked almonds
- 1 tablespoon chopped parsley

HARISSA

- 4 long red chillies
- ½ teaspoon caraway seeds
- ½ teaspoon coriander seeds
- ¾ teaspoon cumin seeds
- ½ teaspoon smoked paprika
- 3 garlic cloves
- ½ teaspoon rock salt
- ½ teaspoon freshly ground black pepper
- 1 tablespoon olive oil
- 1 roasted red capsicum, from a jar (or see page 12)
- juice of ½ lemon

FIG & YOGHURT SAUCE

- 125 g (½ cup) plain yoghurt
- 1 teaspoon tahini
- zest of 1 lemon
- 1 small garlic clove, crushed
- 2 dried figs, finely chopped

ROASTED GARLIC & TOMATO TART

Serves 4

- 3 whole garlic bulbs, unpeeled
- olive oil, for drizzling
- 1 sheet frozen puff pastry, thawed
- milk, for brushing
- 200 g good-quality ricotta
- zest of 1 lemon (optional)
- 300 g cherry tomatoes, cut in half
- small handful thyme sprigs, leaves picked
- balsamic vinegar, for drizzling

— Preheat the oven to 160°C (fan-forced). Line a baking tray with foil.

— Slice the top one-quarter off the garlic bulbs and discard. Place the garlic bulbs on a large square of foil and drizzle with a little olive oil. Wrap the garlic in the foil and roast in the oven for 40 minutes, or until completely soft. Set aside to cool.

— Trim off and reserve about 1 cm from each side of the pastry. Place the pastry on the lined baking tray. Brush the outer edges of the pastry with milk and place the trimmed edges on top, to form a small outer crust during baking.

— Squeeze the flesh from the roasted garlic cloves into a small bowl. Add the ricotta and lemon zest, if using. Season generously with salt and freshly ground black pepper and mix well.

— Spread the ricotta mixture over the pastry, avoiding the border around the edge. Arrange the tomatoes on top, cut side up. Sprinkle with the thyme, drizzle with a little more oil and season with salt and pepper.

— Transfer to the oven and bake for about 30 minutes, or until the pastry is golden brown.

— Serve immediately, with a fresh green salad, and balsamic vinegar to drizzle over the tart.

02

FISH & SHELLFISH

PROSCIUTTO-WRAPPED FISH WITH SICILIAN OLIVES & CHERRY TOMATOES

p.32

SNAPPER IN A SALT CRUST

p.35

SALMON EN CROUTE

p.36

TOMATO & CHORIZO BAKED FISH

p.39

LEMON-ROASTED PRAWNS WITH ROMESCO SAUCE

p.40

LIME, LEMONGRASS & CHILLI ROASTED SALMON

p.43

TRADITIONAL ROAST TROUT WITH HERBS & LEMON

p.44

ROAST CAJUN FISH

p.47

ROASTED SHELLFISH PLATTER

p.48

SALMON EN PAPILLOTE

p.51

PROSCIUTTO-WRAPPED FISH WITH SICILIAN OLIVES & CHERRY TOMATOES

Serves 4

- 400 g mixed cherry tomatoes
- 140 g Sicilian olives
- 1 tablespoon olive oil
- 60 g butter, softened
- 1 lemon, zested, then quartered
- ¾ teaspoon chilli flakes
- 8 slices prosciutto
- 4 x 150–170 g skinless firm white fish fillets, such as rockling, cod or monkfish

— Preheat the oven to 200°C (fan-forced). Lightly oil a roasting tin.

— Toss the tomatoes and olives in the olive oil and season with salt and freshly ground black pepper. Set aside.

— In a small bowl, mix the butter, lemon zest and chilli flakes until combined.

— Lay one slice of prosciutto on a flat surface, and lay another slice on top, overlapping the first on the narrow end. Spoon one-quarter of the butter mixture onto one of the slices and spread evenly. Lay a piece of fish on top of the butter, then roll up the fish in the prosciutto. Place in the roasting tin, seam side down. Repeat with the remaining prosciutto, butter mixture and fish.

— Arrange the tomatoes and olives around the fish, then roast for 8–10 minutes, or until the fish is cooked. The flesh will be opaque all the way through, and will flake easily when a piece is gently tested with a fork.

— Serve immediately with the tomatoes, olives and lemon quarters.

SNAPPER IN A SALT CRUST

Serves 2–3

— Preheat the oven to 180°C (fan-forced).

— To make the salsa verde, put the anchovy and garlic in a small bowl and mash with the back of a fork. Add the capers, mustard and lots of freshly ground black pepper, and mix well. Add the lemon juice and herbs and stir well to combine. Drizzle over the olive oil and season with a little salt. Set aside in the fridge while baking the snapper, for the flavours to infuse.

— Pour the rock salt into a roasting tin large enough to fit your fish. Tip in the egg whites and combine with the rock salt until you have the texture of wet sand. You can add up to 125 ml (½ cup) water, if necessary.

— Peel the rind from the lemon half, avoiding the white pith, and add to the salt slurry along with the coriander seeds. Mix well with your hands, then form a thin layer across the roasting tin where the fish will sit, pushing the remaining salt to the edges. Lay the fish on top and drizzle a little olive oil over it.

— Slice the peeled lemon half and stuff it into the cavity of the fish, along with the herbs. Pile the salt mixture onto the fish until it is completely covered in a layer of salt at least 1 cm thick.

— Transfer to the oven and roast for 25–30 minutes, or until a knife inserted into the thickest part of the fish feels hot to the touch.

— Remove from the oven and allow the fish to rest for 10 minutes.

— Crack the salt crust with a knife and peel back the skin. Serve the fish with the salsa verde, some crusty bread and a simple green salad.

2 kg rock salt

2 free-range egg whites

½ lemon

1 teaspoon coriander seeds, lightly crushed

1–1.2 kg whole white snapper, scaled and cleaned

olive oil, for drizzling

2 rosemary sprigs

3–4 thyme sprigs

crusty bread, to serve

SALSA VERDE

3 large anchovy fillets, finely chopped

2 garlic cloves, finely chopped

1 tablespoon baby capers, drained and rinsed

1 teaspoon dijon mustard

juice of 1 lemon

large handful parsley, finely chopped

small handful basil, finely chopped

small handful dill, chopped (optional)

3–4 tablespoons olive oil

SALMON EN CROUTE

Serves 6

- 600–700 g side of salmon, pin-boned, skin removed
- 1 tablespoon olive oil
- 1 French shallot, finely chopped
- 1 garlic clove, finely chopped
- 250 g spinach, chopped
- 75 g watercress, chopped
- small handful dill, finely chopped
- small handful chives, finely chopped
- 1 dill pickle, finely diced
- 1 tablespoon crème fraîche
- 2 tablespoons dijon mustard
- zest of 1 lemon
- 2 large sheets of puff pastry, or a 500 g block cut in half, both halves rolled out to 5 mm thick
- 1 free-range egg, beaten with 1 tablespoon milk

— Preheat the oven to 170°C (fan-forced).

— If you have a long piece of salmon, cut it in half crossways. If you have a fat, squat piece of salmon, make a deep incision along one side of the fillet, about halfway down, but not all the way through, to 'butterfly' it open, leaving a bit of a hinge.

— Heat the olive oil in a frying pan over medium heat. Add the shallot and garlic and cook, stirring frequently, until lightly browned. Add the spinach and watercress and cook, stirring, until wilted. Remove from the heat and set aside in a sieve to drain.

— Combine the herbs, dill pickle, crème fraîche, mustard and lemon zest in a bowl. Squeeze as much liquid as possible from the spinach mixture then add to the bowl. Season with salt and freshly ground black pepper and stir well to combine.

— Depending on how you've prepared your fish, either fill the salmon cavity or place the spinach mixture on top of one salmon fillet. Place the other fillet on top or close the cavity.

— Place the salmon on top of a pastry sheet. Brush the edges with the egg wash, then place the other pastry sheet on top and seal. You may need to trim the edges if you have too much pastry. Crimp the pastry edges together to seal, then brush all over with the egg wash. Cut shallow slashes across the top of the pastry parcel.

— Transfer to the oven and bake for 30 minutes, or until the pastry is golden.

— Remove from the oven and leave to rest for 10 minutes, then slice and serve with a green salad.

TOMATO & CHORIZO BAKED FISH

Serves 4

— Preheat the oven to 170°C (fan-forced).

— In a heavy-based ovenproof frying pan with a lid, heat the olive oil over medium heat. Add the chorizo, onion and garlic and fry for about 5 minutes, or until the chorizo releases its oil and the onion has softened.

— Add the chilli flakes, paprika, bay leaves, sugar and salt, stirring well. Cook for 1–2 minutes, then stir in the stock and tomatoes. Bring to the boil.

— Put the lid on, then transfer to the oven and cook for 30 minutes.

— Remove from the oven and add the fish, gently submerging the fillets so the sauce coats them all. Return to the oven and cook for a further 8–10 minutes, or until the fish is cooked through.

— Remove from the oven, gently stir in the lemon juice, and scatter the parsley over the fish.

— Serve with crusty bread to mop up the juices, and lemon wedges for squeezing over.

1 tablespoon olive oil
1 chorizo sausage, sliced
1 onion, diced
4 garlic cloves, crushed
1 teaspoon chilli flakes
1 tablespoon smoked paprika
2 bay leaves
1 teaspoon sugar
1 teaspoon salt
400 ml vegetable stock
1 x 400 g tin chopped tomatoes
4 x 150–170 g skinless firm white fish fillets, such as rockling or blue grenadier
2 tablespoons lemon juice
2 tablespoons chopped parsley
crusty bread, to serve
lemon wedges, to serve

LEMON-ROASTED PRAWNS WITH ROMESCO SAUCE

Serves 4

— Preheat the oven to 190°C (fan-forced). Line a tray with baking paper.

— To make the romesco sauce, place the dried ancho chilli in a small bowl of hot water and set aside to soften for 20 minutes.

— Meanwhile, place the tomato halves on the baking tray, cut side up, along with the almonds, garlic cloves and bread. Roast in the oven for 15 minutes, turning the bread, almonds and garlic over now and then.

— Transfer the bread and almonds to a heatproof bowl and continue to roast the tomato and garlic for a further 15 minutes. Add them to the same bowl and set aside to cool.

— Increase the oven temperature to 200°C (fan-forced).

— Drain the ancho chilli, discard the seeds and finely chop the flesh. Transfer to the bowl of a small food processor, along with the roasted tomato, garlic and almonds. Tear the bread into smaller bits and add to the processor with the remaining romesco sauce ingredients. Blitz until you have a fine paste, adding a little more olive oil if necessary. Transfer to a serving bowl.

— Pour the olive oil into a small roasting tin and place in the oven to heat up.

— Combine the prawns, garlic and parsley in a bowl, then carefully transfer to the roasting tin, taking care as the oil will spit. Add the lemon halves, cut side down, and roast in the oven for 8 minutes, or until the prawns are firm and cooked through.

— Transfer the prawns and their juices to a heatproof serving platter. Place the lemon halves on the side for squeezing over.

— Serve immediately, with the romesco sauce for dipping the prawns into. Any left-over romesco will keep in an airtight container in the fridge for up to 5 days.

60 ml (¼ cup) olive oil
16 tiger prawns, kept whole and unpeeled
2 garlic cloves, finely sliced
2 tablespoons chopped parsley
2 lemons, cut in half

ROMESCO SAUCE

1 dried ancho chilli
1 large tomato, cut in half
50 g (⅓ cup) blanched almonds
3 garlic cloves, peeled but left whole
1 slice crusty white bread, about 2 cm thick
80 ml (⅓ cup) olive oil, approximately
1 teaspoon smoked paprika
1½ tablespoons sherry vinegar
small handful parsley, chopped

LIME, LEMONGRASS & CHILLI ROASTED SALMON

Serves 4

— Preheat the oven to 160°C (fan-forced).

— Combine all the ingredients, except the salmon and sesame seeds, in a large bowl. Season well with salt and freshly ground black pepper. Add the salmon fillets and coat them thoroughly with the mixture.

— Cover with plastic wrap and leave in the fridge for 20 minutes for the flavours to infuse.

— Make four foil parcels and place a salmon fillet, skin side down, in each package. Spoon the marinating mixture over each one. Close up the foil parcels and seal tightly, then place on a baking tray.

— Transfer to the oven and roast for 10 minutes, then remove from the oven and leave to rest for 2 minutes.

— Transfer the fish to serving plates. Sprinkle with the toasted sesame seeds, garnish with the coriander leaves, drizzle over any remaining juices from the foil parcels and serve immediately.

large handful coriander, stalks roughly chopped, leaves reserved to garnish

5 garlic cloves, finely chopped

5 cm knob of fresh ginger, finely chopped

2 lemongrass stems, white part only, finely sliced

1 red chilli, finely chopped

1 tablespoon finely grated palm sugar

juice of 2 limes

2 tablespoons fish sauce

4 x 150 g salmon fillets, pin-boned, skin removed

1 tablespoon sesame seeds, lightly toasted

TRADITIONAL ROAST TROUT WITH HERBS & LEMON

Serves 4

— Preheat the oven to 180°C (fan-forced). Line a large baking tray with baking paper.

— Combine all the horseradish cream ingredients in a small bowl and season well with salt and freshly ground black pepper. Taste, then adjust the flavours if necessary. Cover and set aside in the fridge while you prepare the trout.

— Place each fish on the baking tray. Drizzle olive oil over each trout and inside the cavities. Stuff each fish with the herbs and lemon slices. Season well with salt and freshly ground black pepper.

— Transfer to the oven and roast for 20 minutes.

— Remove from the oven and allow the fish to rest for 2 minutes, then transfer to a serving platter.

— Serve the fish in the middle of the table, with the horseradish cream on the side for everyone to help themselves.

2 x 600 g whole rainbow trout, scaled and cleaned

olive oil, for drizzling

small handful thyme

small handful dill

small handful oregano

1 lemon, finely sliced

HORSERADISH CREAM

60 g crème fraîche

60 g (¼ cup) sour cream

2 teaspoons prepared horseradish (from a jar)

2 teaspoons dijon mustard

1 tablespoon finely chopped dill

juice of ½ lemon

ROAST CAJUN FISH

Serves 4

— Preheat the grill to high.

— To make the mango salsa, grill the garlic cloves and chillies for 12–15 minutes, or until well browned and blistered, turning occasionally. Set aside to cool.

— Combine the remaining salsa ingredients in a bowl and season with salt and freshly ground black pepper. Remove the seeds from the chillies, then finely chop the flesh, along with the garlic. Stir through the salsa and check the seasoning. Set aside for 20 minutes for the flavours to infuse.

— Meanwhile, preheat the oven to 180°C (fan-forced). Line a baking tray with foil.

— Combine all the cajun spice mix ingredients in a small bowl, mixing well.

— Brush the fish with the melted butter, then coat well in the cajun spice mix. Heat the olive oil in a large frying pan over high heat and fry the fish for 1 minute on each side, or until blackened but not cooked through.

— Transfer to the baking tray and bake for 6–8 minutes, depending on the thickness of the fish. The fish is cooked when the flesh is opaque all the way through, and flakes easily when gently tested with a fork.

— Serve immediately with the mango salsa.

4 x 150 g thick firm white fish fillets, such as rockling or barramundi

50 g butter, melted

2 tablespoons olive oil

MANGO SALSA

2 garlic cloves, peeled but left whole

2 fresh jalapeño chillies

1 large mango, finely diced

¼ red onion, finely diced

½ red capsicum, finely diced

2 tablespoons chopped coriander

½ avocado, finely diced

juice of 1 lime

CAJUN SPICE MIX

1 tablespoon smoked paprika

2 teaspoons onion powder

2 teaspoons garlic powder

1 teaspoon cayenne pepper

2 teaspoons dried oregano

2 teaspoons dried basil

1½ teaspoons dried thyme

1 teaspoon ground white pepper

1 teaspoon freshly ground black pepper

2 teaspoons salt

ROASTED SHELLFISH PLATTER

Serves 4–6

- 500 g clams (vongole)
- 2 cooked crabs
- 100 ml olive oil
- 75 g butter
- 4 garlic cloves, crushed
- large handful parsley, roughly chopped
- 1 raw lobster tail, sliced in half lengthways
- 12 large tiger prawns, kept whole and unpeeled
- 1 kg mussels, scrubbed well, beards removed
- crusty white bread, to serve
- 2 lemons, cut into wedges

SAFFRON MAYONNAISE

- pinch of saffron threads
- 1 large free-range egg yolk
- ½ teaspoon dijon mustard
- up to 160 ml neutral-flavoured oil, such as grapeseed or canola
- juice of 1 lemon

— Soak the clams in a large bowl of cold water for 1 hour to remove any grit or sand. Meanwhile, make the saffron mayonnaise. Soak the saffron threads in 1 tablespoon hot water for about 10 minutes. Place the egg yolk, mustard and a large pinch of salt into the bowl of a small food processor. Process for about 1½ minutes, or until light and airy. With the motor running, slowly add the oil — drop by drop at first, then in a thin, steady stream, until you have a thick, glossy mayonnaise. Combine the lemon juice and saffron water and slowly pour the mixture in, processing until well combined. Transfer to the fridge for the mayonnaise to chill and firm up.

— When you're ready to start cooking, preheat the oven to 210°C (fan-forced). Prepare the crabs by firmly lifting the base of the outer shell until it comes away completely. Rinse away the greyish material, snap off the 'apron' and mandibles at either end of the crab, and remove the gills in the middle. Slice each crab in half and use a meat mallet or rolling pin to smash the large front legs.

— Pour 60 ml (¼ cup) of the olive oil into a large roasting tin and place in the oven to heat up.

— In a small saucepan, melt the butter and remaining oil over low heat and add the garlic and parsley. Set aside.

— Place the lobster tail halves, flesh side down, in the hot roasting tin, along with the prawns. Roast in the oven for 3 minutes.

— Meanwhile, drain the clams and rinse well. Tip the clams and mussels into another large roasting tin and add 60 ml (¼ cup) water. Drizzle over half the melted garlic butter and place in the oven.

— Remove the other roasting tin from the oven and flip the lobster and prawns over. Add the crab to the roasting tin and drizzle with the remaining melted garlic butter. Return to the oven and roast for a further 6–8 minutes, turning the prawns, mussels and clams every couple of minutes, until the mussels and clams have opened, and the lobster is cooked through.

— Transfer the shellfish to a large serving platter, then drizzle with all the juices from both roasting tins. Serve immediately, with crusty white bread for mopping up the juice, and lemon wedges for squeezing over.

SALMON EN PAPILLOTE

Serves 4

4 medium-sized boiling potatoes
2 garlic cloves, finely sliced
zest and juice of 2 lemons
2 tablespoons white wine
60 ml (¼ cup) olive oil
4 x 150 g salmon fillets, pin-boned, skin removed
1 large fennel bulb, sliced as finely as possible
8 cornichons, cut in half lengthways
a few dill or fennel fronds, roughly chopped

— Place the potatoes in a saucepan and cover with cold water. Season with salt and bring to the boil. Simmer for 8 minutes, or until just tender, then drain and set aside to cool slightly.

— Meanwhile, preheat the oven to 180°C (fan-forced). Tear off four large sheets of baking paper and fold them into loose parcels.

— Combine the garlic, lemon zest, lemon juice, wine and olive oil in a small screw-top jar. Season well with salt and freshly ground black pepper. Seal the jar and shake well.

— Peel the potatoes, if you like, then finely slice. Arrange the slices on the base of each parcel. Place a salmon fillet on top of each potato layer, then scatter with the fennel, cornichons and dill or fennel fronds. Give the dressing a good shake again and drizzle over the fish. Seal the parcels, making sure they are watertight.

— Place the parcels on a baking tray, then into the oven. Bake for 12–15 minutes, or until the fish is just cooked through and flakes easily when gently tested with a fork.

— Serve immediately, with a green salad on the side.

03

POULTRY

MOROCCAN-SPICED ROAST CHICKEN WITH PRESERVED LEMON
p.54

ROLLED TURKEY BREAST WITH LEMON & HERB STUFFING
p.57

MUSHROOM-STUFFED CHICKEN BREASTS WITH GARLIC CREAM SAUCE
p.58

ROAST DUCK WITH MAPLE & BALSAMIC GLAZE
p.61

CHICKEN WITH 40 CLOVES OF GARLIC & LEMON GARLIC GRAVY
p.62

ROAST QUAIL WITH BAKED FIGS, FETA & PISTACHIOS
p.65

ROAST GOOSE WITH CHESTNUT & APPLE STUFFING
p.66

SPICY ROASTED CHICKEN WITH BLUE CHEESE SAUCE
p.69

ROAST DUCK WITH ORANGE & CHERRY SAUCE
p.70

ROAST CHICKEN WITH WALNUT & SAGE STUFFING & PARSNIP GRAVY
p.72

SPICED POUSSIN WITH HERBED YOGHURT
p.77

ROAST TURKEY WITH SPICY CRANBERRY SAUCE
p.78

CHICKEN IN COCONUT MILK
p.82

MOROCCAN-SPICED ROAST CHICKEN WITH PRESERVED LEMON

Serves 4

— Preheat the oven to 180°C (fan-forced).

— Cut the capsicum into eight even-sized pieces. Remove and discard the seeds and membrane, then place in a bowl with the whole potatoes and shallots. Add the olive oil and toss until the vegetables are coated. Season with salt and freshly ground black pepper and set aside.

— In a small bowl, mix together all the spiced lemon butter ingredients until well combined.

— Use a spoon or your fingers to very gently separate the chicken skin from the breast and the top of the thighs. Push three-quarters of the spiced butter under the skin, smoothing it out to ensure it is evenly distributed. Rub the remaining butter on the outside of the skin.

— Place the chicken in a roasting tin, transfer to the oven and roast for 20 minutes.

— Add the potatoes and shallots to the roasting tin and roast for a further 40 minutes. Add the capsicum and roast for a final 20 minutes; the chicken needs to roast for 1 hour 20 minutes in total.

— Leaving the vegetables in the roasting tin, transfer the chicken to a plate, cover loosely with foil and leave to rest for 15 minutes.

— Meanwhile, add the green beans to the roasting tin and roast for 15 minutes.

— Serve the chicken drizzled with any juices from the roasting tin, with the roasted vegetables alongside. Steamed couscous would be a lovely accompaniment.

1 large red capsicum

600 g new potatoes, scrubbed

4 French shallots, peeled

1 tablespoon olive oil

1 whole free-range chicken, about 1.5–1.7 kg

250 g green beans

SPICED LEMON BUTTER

60 g butter, softened

½ teaspoon freshly ground black pepper

½ teaspoon salt

¼ teaspoon sumac

½ teaspoon ground coriander

¼ teaspoon ground cinnamon

½ teaspoon ground cumin

½ teaspoon smoked paprika

½ teaspoon chilli flakes

½ preserved lemon, rinsed, flesh discarded, rind finely diced

ROLLED TURKEY BREAST WITH LEMON & HERB STUFFING

Serves 10–12

— Preheat the oven to 160°C (fan-forced).

— To make the stuffing, heat the butter and olive oil in a large frying pan over medium heat. Add the onion and garlic and cook for 6–8 minutes, or until the onion is softened. Transfer to a large bowl and set aside to cool, then add the remaining stuffing ingredients and mix well.

— Lay the turkey breast, skin side down, on a chopping board. Using a sharp knife, cut horizontally through the thickest part of the breast, nearly to the other side, but not all the way through. Open the fillet out like a book.

— Press the stuffing onto the breast, then roll up the turkey to enclose the stuffing. Get someone to help you tie the turkey with kitchen string every 3 cm to secure the roll, then place on a roasting rack in a roasting tin. Brush the entire surface of the turkey with the olive oil.

— Transfer to the oven and roast for 2 hours, or until the turkey is golden brown, and the juices run clear when you poke a skewer into the centre, or a meat thermometer registers 75°C when you test the meat in several places.

— Remove the turkey from the oven, cover loosely with foil and leave to rest for 15 minutes. Save the roasting tin juices for making a gravy to serve with the turkey, if desired, or for another use.

— Remove and discard the string from the turkey, then carve into slices. Serve scattered with sage, and with gravy, if desired.

— The Spicy cranberry sauce from the roast turkey recipe on page 78 is also delicious here.

- 1 x 2 kg turkey breast fillet (unfilled turkey breast roll)
- 1 tablespoon olive oil
- sage leaves, to garnish

LEMON & HERB STUFFING

- 20 g butter
- 1 tablespoon olive oil
- 1 onion, finely chopped
- 2 garlic cloves, crushed
- 200 g pork and fennel sausages, removed from their casings
- finely grated zest of 1 lemon
- 2 tablespoons shredded sage leaves
- 45 g (¼ cup) raw unsalted pistachio nuts
- large handful parsley, chopped
- 140 g (2 cups) fresh sourdough breadcrumbs
- 1 free-range egg, beaten

TIP

You may need to order a turkey breast fillet from your local poultry supplier or butcher. Allow 1 hour of cooking at 160°C (fan-forced) for the first 1 kg of rolled turkey breast and stuffing, then 20 minutes per 1 kg thereafter.

MUSHROOM-STUFFED CHICKEN BREASTS WITH GARLIC CREAM SAUCE

Serves 4

— Heat 1 tablespoon of the olive oil in a frying pan over medium heat and fry the mushrooms for 3–4 minutes, or until cooked. Transfer to a bowl, along with the cheese and breadcrumbs. Season with salt and freshly ground black pepper, mix together and set aside to cool.

— Preheat the oven to 180°C (fan-forced). Lay a chicken breast flat on a chopping board, with the smooth round side facing downwards. Being careful not to slice all the way through, use a sharp knife to make a small cut along the join where the tenderloin meets the breast, to flatten slightly. Now push the blade from the side near the join into the thickest part of the breast, and draw downwards, to create a pocket within the breast. Gently push one-quarter of the mushroom stuffing into the pocket, then pull the tenderloin over the join, creating a 'lid' for the opening. Wrap a slice of bacon around the stuffed breast, securing with a toothpick if needed. Repeat with the remaining chicken breasts, stuffing and bacon.

— Heat the remaining oil in a large frying pan, then brown the bacon-wrapped chicken breasts for about 2 minutes on each side.

— Transfer to a roasting tin and roast for 30–40 minutes, or until the internal temperature of the chicken reaches 75°C on a meat thermometer.

— While the chicken is in the oven, make the garlic cream sauce. Heat the olive oil in a frying pan over medium heat and fry the garlic for 1 minute. Increase the heat to high, add the wine and bring to the boil. Reduce the heat to medium and simmer until the liquid has reduced by half. Stir in the cream and continue to simmer until the liquid has again reduced by half, and the sauce has thickened. Allow the chicken to rest for 5 minutes, then slice each breast into rounds. Serve with the garlic cream sauce.

2 tablespoons olive oil
220 g mushrooms, diced
100 g cheddar, grated
55 g (⅔ cup) fresh breadcrumbs
4 free-range chicken breast fillets
4 slices middle bacon

GARLIC CREAM SAUCE

1 tablespoon olive oil
3 garlic cloves, crushed
250 ml (1 cup) white wine
250 ml (1 cup) cream

ROAST DUCK WITH MAPLE & BALSAMIC GLAZE

Serves 4

- 1 x 2 kg whole duck
- 1 lemon, cut in half
- 2 sage sprigs
- 4 rosemary sprigs
- 250 ml (1 cup) duck or chicken stock
- 2 teaspoons cornflour

MAPLE & BALSAMIC GLAZE

- 60 g butter
- 125 ml (½ cup) maple syrup
- 60 ml (¼ cup) good-quality balsamic vinegar

— Preheat the oven to 170°C (fan-forced). Remove the neck from the duck and trim the wings to the second joint. Open the vent at the leg end and drain any liquid from the cavity. Dry the skin with paper towel and season the duck, inside and out, with salt and freshly ground black pepper. Place the lemon halves, sage sprigs and one of the rosemary sprigs in the cavity.

— Place the duck on a roasting rack in a roasting tin. Transfer to the oven and roast for 30 minutes. Meanwhile, make the maple and balsamic glaze. Combine the butter, maple syrup and vinegar in a small saucepan over high heat. Bring to the boil, then reduce the heat and simmer for 5–6 minutes, stirring occasionally, until slightly thickened. Season with salt and pepper.

— Tie the remaining three rosemary sprigs together at the woody end with kitchen string, to make a glazing brush. Remove the duck from the oven and brush all over with the glaze, using the rosemary sprigs as a brush. Return the duck to the oven and brush with more glaze every 20 minutes for the next hour, or until cooked through and well glazed, reserving any left-over glaze for the gravy.

— Transfer the duck to a warm plate, cover loosely with foil and leave to rest for 20 minutes. While the duck is resting, make a gravy. Pour off most of the duck fat from the roasting tin and save for another use, such as roasting potatoes. Place the roasting tin over medium heat and add the stock. Scrape the base of the pan with a spoon to dislodge all the good bits, then simmer for 5 minutes, or until reduced slightly. In a small bowl, mix the cornflour to a smooth paste with a little water. Add to the stock with any left-over glaze, whisking until combined. Simmer, whisking, for 1–2 minutes, or until slightly thickened. Strain if necessary. Carve the duck and serve with the gravy.

TIP

The approximate roasting time for a whole duck is 40 minutes per 1 kg.

CHICKEN WITH 40 CLOVES OF GARLIC & LEMON GARLIC GRAVY

Serves 4

8 free-range chicken thighs, skin on and bone in

1 tablespoon olive oil

20 g butter

190 ml (¾ cup) white wine

250 ml (1 cup) chicken stock

40 garlic cloves, unpeeled

8 thyme sprigs

1 bay leaf

1 lemon, cut in half

1 tablespoon plain flour

crusty bread, to serve

— Preheat the oven to 160°C (fan-forced).

— Pat the chicken thighs dry with paper towel. Place a flameproof casserole dish, large enough to fit all the chicken in a single layer, over medium–high heat; you'll need one with a tight-fitting lid. Add the olive oil and butter, then add half the chicken, skin side down, and brown well for about 5 minutes. Turn the chicken and brown the other side for about 3–4 minutes. Remove to a plate and brown the remaining chicken pieces in the same way, then add them to the plate.

— Drain the excess fat from the dish. Reduce the heat, add the wine to the pan and leave to simmer for 1–2 minutes.

— Stir in the stock, scatter in a handful of the garlic cloves, then return all the chicken to the pan, fitting it in snugly in a single layer. Add the thyme sprigs, bay leaf and lemon halves, then tuck the remaining garlic cloves in around the chicken.

— Remove the casserole dish from the heat. Cover with a double layer of foil, tightly sealing the edges, then place the lid on. Transfer to the oven and roast for 1¼ hours.

— Remove the dish from the oven. Transfer the chicken and garlic to a plate, leaving about 10 cloves of garlic and all the juices in the dish. Loosely cover the chicken with foil to keep warm.

— Using a spoon, press down on the garlic cloves in the casserole dish to release them from their skins. Discard the skins, and mash the garlic into the juices.

— Place the dish back over medium–high heat. Mix 2–3 tablespoons of the juices with the flour until smooth, then add to the dish and stir well, cooking for a few minutes until the gravy has thickened. Remove from the heat and return the chicken and garlic cloves to the dish. Serve with crusty bread, to mop up all the juices and to spread the garlic over.

ROAST QUAIL WITH BAKED FIGS, FETA & PISTACHIOS

Serves 4–6

— Preheat the oven to 160°C (fan-forced). Line a large roasting tin with baking paper.

— Heat a large chargrill pan over high heat. Drizzle the figs with a little olive oil and place on the hot pan, cut side down. Cook for 1–2 minutes, or until marked, then set aside.

— Season the quail with salt and freshly ground black pepper and brush with olive oil. Working in batches if necessary, chargrill the quail, skin side down, for 3–4 minutes, or until well browned, then turn and cook the other side for a further 1 minute.

— Transfer to the roasting tin, skin side up, along with the figs. Drizzle all over with the pomegranate molasses and roast for 5–8 minutes, or until the quail is cooked through.

— Transfer the quail to a warm plate and cover loosely with foil to rest for a few minutes.

— Serve the quail with the figs, scattered with the feta, pistachios and pomegranate seeds. Drizzle with any pan juices and a little extra pomegranate molasses if you like.

6 fresh figs, cut in half

olive oil, for drizzling and brushing

6 quail, butterflied

2 tablespoons pomegranate molasses, plus extra to serve

100 g (⅔ cup) crumbled feta

2 tablespoons pistachio nuts, roughly chopped or slivered

fresh pomegranate seeds, to serve

TIP

To butterfly the quail, cut along both sides of the spine with kitchen scissors and discard the backbone (or save for making stock). Open the quail out, skin side up, and press gently with the heel of your hand to flatten. Tuck the wing tips underneath.

ROAST GOOSE WITH CHESTNUT & APPLE STUFFING

Serves 6

— Preheat the oven to 200°C (fan-forced). Fold the wings under the goose. Open the vent at the leg end and drain any liquid from the cavity. Remove any excess fat and cut off the neck. Dry the skin with paper towel and season the goose, inside and out, with salt and pepper. Rub the seasoning into the skin, then rub the goose all over with the olive oil. Place the lemon halves, rosemary and sage sprigs in the cavity.

— Place the goose on a roasting rack in a roasting tin and roast for 20 minutes. Meanwhile, start making the stuffing. Heat the butter and oil in a large frying pan over medium heat. Add the onion and garlic and cook for 6–8 minutes, or until the onion is softened. Transfer to a large bowl and set aside to cool.

— When the goose has roasted for 20 minutes, reduce the oven temperature to 160°C (fan-forced). Roast for a further 2 hours 20 minutes, or until the legs pull away easily, or a meat thermometer registers 75°C when you test the meat in several places.

— About 15 minutes before the goose is done, add the remaining stuffing ingredients to the sautéed onion mixture. Mix well and season to taste. Butter a small loaf tin and either spoon the stuffing into it, or form it into a log shape on a piece of baking paper and place it in the tin. Drizzle with a little goose fat from the main roasting tin.

— The stuffing will take about 40 minutes to cook through, so add it to the oven about 10 minutes before the goose is done. At this time you could also add any root vegetables you'd like to roast and serve along with the goose.

— When the goose has finished cooking, transfer it to a warm plate, cover loosely with foil and leave to rest for 30 minutes. Meanwhile, leave the stuffing in the oven for a further 30 minutes, or until lightly browned and just firm to touch. Carve the goose and serve with the stuffing.

1 x 3.5–4 kg whole goose

1 tablespoon olive oil

1 lemon, cut in half

1 rosemary sprig

2 sage sprigs

CHESTNUT & APPLE STUFFING LOAF

20 g butter

1 tablespoon olive oil

1 onion, finely chopped

2 garlic cloves, crushed

200 g pork sausages, removed from their casings

140 g (2 cups) fresh sourdough breadcrumbs

70 g (½ cup) frozen prepared chestnuts, thawed and roughly chopped

1 apple, grated

2 tablespoons shredded sage leaves

large handful parsley, chopped

finely grated zest of 1 orange

1 free-range egg, beaten

SPICY ROASTED CHICKEN WITH BLUE CHEESE SAUCE

Serves 4

- 100 g (⅔ cup) plain flour
- 2 teaspoons garlic powder
- 2 teaspoons salt
- 1 teaspoon freshly ground black pepper
- 1 teaspoon smoked paprika
- 1.5 kg chicken pieces, a mix of wingettes and drumettes
- 100 ml hot sauce, such as Tabasco
- 75 g butter, melted

BLUE CHEESE SAUCE

- 125 g (½ cup) sour cream
- 130 g whole-egg mayonnaise
- 1 large garlic clove, crushed
- 100 g stilton
- 100 g mild blue cheese

— Preheat the oven to 200°C (fan-forced).

— Place the flour, garlic powder, salt, pepper and paprika in a large zip-lock bag. Working in batches, toss the chicken pieces in the bag, ensuring each is evenly coated. Remove from the bag, shaking off the excess, and place on a roasting rack over a baking tray.

— Transfer to the oven and roast for 35 minutes.

— When the chicken is nearly ready, place all the ingredients for the blue cheese sauce in the bowl of a small food processor and process into a smooth sauce. Transfer to a small bowl and set aside until ready to serve.

— When the chicken is done, remove from the oven. In a large bowl, mix the hot sauce with the melted butter, then add the chicken pieces and toss to coat.

— Serve immediately, with the blue cheese sauce.

ROAST DUCK WITH ORANGE & CHERRY SAUCE

Serves 4

- 4 duck leg quarters
- olive oil, for pan-frying
- 125 ml (½ cup) dry Jerez sherry or apera
- 300 g fresh or frozen cherries, pitted and halved
- shredded zest of 1 orange
- 125 ml (½ cup) orange juice
- 1 teaspoon light soy sauce

— Preheat the oven to 160°C (fan-forced).

— Season the duck leg quarters with salt and freshly ground black pepper. Heat a heavy-based flameproof roasting tin over medium heat, then add a splash of olive oil. Cook the duck for 5–6 minutes on each side, or until very well browned all over, using tongs to tilt the legs and brown the sides as well.

— Carefully tilt the roasting tin and spoon out any excess fat, saving it for another use, such as roasting potatoes.

— Transfer to the oven and roast for 45–50 minutes, or until the duck is tender and the skin is crisp.

— Transfer the leg quarters to a plate, cover loosely with foil and leave to rest in a warm place for 15 minutes.

— While the duck is resting, make the sauce. Carefully pour the excess fat from the roasting tin, adding it to the previously collected fat. Place the roasting tin back over medium heat and add the sherry, scraping the bottom of the tin to loosen any browned goodness from the duck. Simmer for 2–3 minutes, or until reduced slightly. Add the cherries, orange zest and orange juice and simmer, partially covered, for 10 minutes, or until the cherries are soft and collapsing. Stir in the soy sauce and cook, uncovered, for a further 2–3 minutes, or until slightly thickened. Season to taste.

— Serve the duck with the cherry sauce. Mashed potatoes and steamed greens make great accompaniments to this dish.

ROAST CHICKEN WITH WALNUT & SAGE STUFFING & PARSNIP GRAVY

Serves 4

- 1 carrot
- 1 large onion
- 2 parsnips
- 2 celery stalks
- 4 garlic cloves, unpeeled
- 75 g butter, softened
- 1 teaspoon chopped sage
- 1 teaspoon chopped parsley
- 1 free-range whole chicken, about 1.5–1.7 kg
- 170 ml (⅔ cup) white wine
- 250 ml (1 cup) chicken stock, plus a little extra
- 1 tablespoon plain flour

— Preheat the oven to 180°C (fan-forced).

— Peel the carrot, onion and parsnips. Roughly chop them, along with the celery, and place in a roasting tin with the unpeeled garlic cloves.

— Put 60 g of the butter in a small bowl. Add the sage and parsley, season with salt and freshly ground black pepper and mix well with a fork.

— Use a spoon or your fingers to very gently separate the chicken skin from the breast and the top of the thighs. Push three-quarters of the herb butter under the skin, smoothing it out to ensure it is evenly distributed. Rub the remaining herb butter on the outside of the skin, and season with salt and pepper.

— Place the chicken in the roasting tin, on top of the vegetables. Transfer to the oven and roast for 40 minutes.

— Meanwhile, make the stuffing. Melt the butter in a frying pan over medium heat, then fry the bacon, onion and sage for about 5 minutes, or until the onion is softened and the bacon is cooked.

— Transfer to a bowl, add the breadcrumbs, walnuts and parsley, season well with salt and freshly ground black pepper, and stir to combine. Add the eggs and mix well. Using your hands, shape the mixture into 12 evenly sized balls, and place on a baking tray lined with baking paper until ready to cook.

— Once the chicken has roasted for 40 minutes, remove from the oven and add the wine and stock to the roasting tin.

— Roast for a further 40 minutes, or until the chicken reaches an internal temperature of 75°C when tested with a meat thermometer, adding the tray of stuffing balls to the oven with 5 minutes to go.

— Remove the roasting tin from the oven. Transfer the chicken to a plate, cover loosely with foil and leave to rest for 15 minutes while the stuffing finishes cooking, and you make the gravy.

— Strain the juices from the roasting tin, into a measuring jug.

— Take the parsnips and garlic from the roasting tin. Peel the garlic. Purée the parsnips and garlic with the strained roasting tin juices, using a hand-held stick blender or a blender.

— Strain the liquid back into the measuring jug, adding a little extra stock if needed to top up the liquid level to 375 ml (1½ cups).

— Discard any solids remaining in the roasting tin. Melt the remaining butter in the roasting tin over low heat, then add the flour and stir until it becomes a smooth paste. Cook for 2–3 minutes, then add the stock gradually, stirring until you have a thickened sauce, ensuring any bits stuck to the bottom of the tin are scraped off and mixed into the gravy. Stir in any juices that have collected from the chicken during resting.

— When ready to serve, carve the chicken and serve with the stuffing and gravy.

WALNUT & SAGE STUFFING

- 40 g butter
- 200 g bacon, diced
- 1 large onion, diced
- 14 sage leaves, shredded
- 240 g (3 cups) fresh breadcrumbs
- 100 g (1 cup) walnuts, chopped
- 3 teaspoons chopped parsley
- 2 free-range eggs, beaten

Roast chicken with walnut & sage stuffing & parsnip gravy

SPICED POUSSIN WITH HERBED YOGHURT

Serves 4

— Using kitchen string, truss the legs of each poussin together.

— In a small bowl, mix together the spices, olive oil, yoghurt, garlic and lemon juice until well combined. Massage the mixture over each poussin, then transfer to the fridge to marinate for 2 hours.

— Preheat the oven to 160°C (fan-forced).

— Place the poussin in a roasting tin and roast for 45–55 minutes, or until the juices run clear when tested with a skewer inserted into the thickest part of the thigh.

— Remove from the oven, cover lightly with foil and leave to rest for 10 minutes.

— Meanwhile, combine all the herbed yoghurt ingredients in a small bowl, mixing well.

— Serve the poussin with the herbed yoghurt.

4 poussin, weighing about 500 g each
2 teaspoons ground cumin
1 tablespoon ground turmeric
½ teaspoon ground coriander
½ teaspoon garam masala
½ teaspoon salt
½ teaspoon freshly ground black pepper
2 tablespoons olive oil
125 g (½ cup) Greek-style yoghurt
2 garlic cloves, crushed
juice of 1 lemon

HERBED YOGHURT

250 g (1 cup) Greek-style yoghurt
1 tablespoon chopped mint
1 tablespoon chopped coriander leaves
1 tablespoon chopped parsley
1 garlic clove, crushed

ROAST TURKEY WITH SPICY CRANBERRY SAUCE

Serves 8–10

- 1 x 5 kg turkey, fresh or frozen then fully thawed
- 1 teaspoon salt
- 50 g butter, melted

CHORIZO CRANBERRY STUFFING

- 40 g butter
- 2 tablespoons olive oil
- 2 onions, finely chopped
- 3 garlic cloves, crushed
- ½ teaspoon hot smoked paprika
- 1 fresh chorizo sausage, removed from its casing
- 500 ml (2 cups) chicken stock
- 350 g thick sourdough bread, torn into 1.5 cm chunks
- 120 g (1 cup) roughly chopped pecans
- 125 g (½ cup) roughly chopped pitted prunes
- 70 g (½ cup) dried cranberries
- 50 g (½ cup) finely grated parmesan
- large handful parsley, chopped

— To make the stuffing, heat the butter and olive oil in a large frying pan over medium heat. Add the onion, garlic, paprika and sausage meat. Cook for 5–8 minutes, or until the onion is softened and the sausage meat cooked through.

— Transfer to a large bowl and set aside to cool. Add 375 ml (1½ cups) of the stock, then the remaining stuffing ingredients. Mix well, then set aside to soak for 10 minutes. (If making ahead, the stuffing can be refrigerated for up to 1 day.)

— Preheat the oven to 160°C (fan-forced). Place a roasting rack in a large roasting tin, and lightly grease a 1.5 litre (6 cup) baking dish.

— Tuck the wings under the turkey, sprinkle the salt into the main cavity and tie the legs together with kitchen string. Open up the neck cavity and work your fingertips between the skin and the breast meat, to separate them. Push about 1 cup of the cooled stuffing under the skin, to cover about half of the breast area, to protect it from drying out. Secure the opening with a skewer.

— Spoon the remaining stuffing into the greased baking dish, evenly pour the remaining stock over, then cover and refrigerate until required.

— Brush the turkey skin all over with the melted butter and season lightly with salt and freshly ground black pepper. Place the turkey on the roasting rack in the roasting tin, then add 500 ml (2 cups) water to the tin. Cover firstly with a large sheet of baking paper, then securely with foil.

— Transfer carefully to the oven and roast for 2 hours.

— Carefully remove the foil and baking paper. Add the stuffing to the oven and roast the turkey and stuffing for a further 1 hour, or until the stuffing and turkey skin are golden, and the turkey juices run clear when tested with a skewer inserted into the thickest part of the thigh; a meat thermometer should register 75°C when you test the meat in several different places.

— Remove the turkey from the oven, cover loosely with foil and leave to rest for 30 minutes before carving. Save the roasting tin juices for making a gravy to serve with the turkey, if desired, or for another use.

— While the turkey is resting, make the cranberry sauce. Heat the olive oil in a saucepan over medium heat and cook the onion for 5 minutes, or until softened, stirring occasionally. Add the remaining ingredients and bring to the boil, stirring occasionally. Reduce the heat to medium-low and simmer for 10 minutes, or until the fruit is soft, and the sauce has slightly thickened. Season to taste, adding a little more sugar if necessary; sometimes cranberries can be a little bitter. Remove from the heat and set aside to cool.

— Carve the turkey and serve with the stuffing and cranberry sauce.

SPICY CRANBERRY SAUCE

- 1 tablespoon olive oil
- 1 onion, finely chopped
- 500 g (4½ cups) cranberries, fresh or frozen
- 2 apples, peeled, cored and chopped
- 110 g (½ cup) brown sugar, approximately
- ½ teaspoon chilli flakes
- 80 ml (⅓ cup) dry Jerez sherry, apera or apple juice

TIP

For every 1 kg of turkey, allow 35–40 minutes of cooking time at 160°C (fan-forced) – about 3 hours for a 5 kg turkey. The cranberry sauce can be made 2–3 days ahead and refrigerated; it yields about 2½ cups.

CHICKEN IN COCONUT MILK

Serves 4

- 1 free-range whole chicken, about 1.5–1.7 kg
- 60 ml (¼ cup) olive oil
- grated zest and juice of ½ lime
- 400 ml coconut milk
- 250 ml (1 cup) chicken stock
- 2 teaspoons grated palm sugar
- small knob of fresh ginger, peeled and thickly sliced
- 1 lemongrass stem, trimmed and bashed
- 4 garlic cloves, sliced
- ½ teaspoon chilli flakes
- coriander, to serve

— Preheat the oven to 180°C (fan-forced).

— Cut the chicken into 8 pieces.

— Heat a large flameproof casserole dish over medium–high heat. Add the olive oil and brown the chicken on all sides, for about 5–6 minutes.

— Turn off the heat, then drain off and discard the oil from the pan.

— Sprinkle the lime zest and juice over the chicken. Mix together the coconut milk, stock, sugar, ginger, lemongrass, garlic and chilli flakes and pour over the chicken.

— Put the lid on, transfer to the oven and roast for 15 minutes. Baste the chicken with the sauce, put the lid back on and bake for a further 15 minutes.

— Remove the lid and cook for a further 15 minutes, or until the skin is nicely browned and the internal temperature of the chicken reaches 75°C on a meat thermometer.

— Transfer the chicken to a serving dish. Pour the sauce over the chicken, garnish with coriander and serve. Steamed jasmine rice would be a lovely accompaniment.

04

MEAT

ROAST STUFFED PORK
WITH APPLES TWO WAYS
p.86

BEEF CHEEKS
IN RED WINE SAUCE
p.89

SLOW-ROASTED GREEK
LAMB WITH POTATOES
p.90

PORK KNUCKLE
WITH APPLE SAUCE
& SAUERKRAUT
p.92

SLOW-ROASTED
RABBIT STEW
p.96

CRISPY PORK BELLY
WITH FIVE-SPICE
& DIPPING SAUCE
p.99

BOEUF EN CROUTE
WITH RED WINE JUS
p.100

MINI LAMB ROASTS
WITH CHIMICHURRI
p.104

STICKY ROAST PORK
RIBS WITH SLAW
p.107

BEEF POT ROAST
p.108

MUSTARD-GLAZED
ROAST LEG OF HAM WITH
PEACH SALSA
p.111

ROAST BEEF RIBS
WITH PARSNIPS &
HORSERADISH CREAM
p.112

LAMB SHANKS WITH
CANNELLINI BEANS
p.115

ROAST STUFFED PORK WITH APPLES TWO WAYS

Serves 8

- 1 rolled pork loin, weighing about 2 kg
- 2 tablespoons olive oil, plus extra for brushing
- sea salt flakes, for sprinkling
- 6 granny smith apples

SAGE & APPLE STUFFING

- 2 Italian-style sausages, about 250 g in total
- 1 tablespoon olive oil
- 1 onion, diced
- 1 celery stalk, chopped
- 2 garlic cloves, crushed
- 2 granny smith apples, finely diced
- 1 teaspoon smoked paprika
- 120 g (1½ cups) fresh breadcrumbs
- ½ teaspoon salt
- ½ teaspoon freshly ground black pepper
- 12 sage leaves, roughly chopped

— Untie the rolled loin, place it on a flat surface and use a sharp knife to score the skin. Place the pork on a rack over the sink, skin side up, and pour boiling water over the skin to open up the cuts. Dry with paper towel, then place the pork in the fridge to dry for 3–4 hours, or overnight.

— When you're ready to start cooking, remove the pork from the fridge and leave for 30 minutes to bring it to room temperature. Meanwhile, preheat the oven to 210°C (fan-forced), and make the stuffing.

— Remove the sausages from their casings and chop the meat. Heat the olive oil in a frying pan over medium–high heat, then fry the sausage meat until cooked, mashing it with a wooden spoon as you go to ensure it breaks up. Remove from the frying pan and place in a mixing bowl.

— Reduce the heat to medium and add the onion, celery and garlic to the pan. Fry for about 10 minutes, or until soft and translucent, but not browned, then add to the sausage mixture and allow to cool. Add the diced apple, along with the remaining stuffing ingredients, and mix well.

— Lay the pork flat, skin side down. Use a sharp knife to partially slice through the thick meaty end, and gently open it up, so that the loin is now longer and flatter, ready for stuffing. Lay the stuffing evenly over one-third of one end of the pork, then tightly roll up the rest of the loin, securing it in place using kitchen string at even intervals down the length of the loin.

— Place the pork in a roasting tin. Rub the olive oil over the skin, then season generously with salt flakes. Transfer to the oven and roast for 30 minutes, then reduce the heat to 160°C (fan-forced) and roast for a further 30 minutes.

— Rub the whole apples with a splash of olive oil and season with salt and freshly ground black pepper. Add the apples to the roasting tin and continue to roast for a further 30 minutes. Remove from the oven, cover loosely with foil and set aside to rest for 15–20 minutes before serving.

BEEF CHEEKS IN RED WINE SAUCE

Serves 4

- 2 tablespoons plain flour
- 800 g beef cheeks (4 cheeks)
- 2 tablespoons olive oil
- 2 onions, cut into chunks
- 6 garlic cloves, sliced
- 1 large carrot, thickly sliced
- 2 celery stalks, thickly sliced
- 3 rosemary sprigs
- 3 sage sprigs
- 2 tablespoons tomato paste
- 500 ml (2 cups) red wine
- 350 ml beef stock

— Preheat the oven to 130°C (fan-forced).

— Put the flour in a zip-lock bag and season well with salt and freshly ground black pepper. Toss the beef cheeks in the flour, ensuring they are coated evenly, then shake off the excess.

— Heat the olive oil in a flameproof casserole dish over medium–high heat. Working in batches if necessary, brown the cheeks well, for about 2 minutes on each side. Remove and set aside.

— Reduce the heat to medium, add the onion, garlic, carrot and celery to the pan and fry for 4–5 minutes, or until the vegetables have softened. Add the rosemary, sage and tomato paste, stir to combine, then cook for a further 1–2 minutes.

— Pour in the wine, stirring well to loosen any bits that have stuck to the bottom of the dish. Allow the wine to come to the boil, then simmer for 3–4 minutes. Stir in the stock, bring back to the boil, then turn off the heat.

— Return the beef cheeks to the dish, pushing them down so they are covered by the sauce. Put the lid on, then transfer to the oven to bake for 2½–3 hours, turning the cheeks once or twice so they cook evenly.

— Serve with mashed potato and steamed green beans.

SLOW-ROASTED GREEK LAMB WITH POTATOES

Serves 6

- 1 leg of lamb, weighing about 2 kg
- 1 small bunch oregano
- 5 garlic cloves, peeled and sliced in half lengthways
- 2 tablespoons olive oil
- 125 ml (½ cup) white wine
- 1 lemon, quartered
- 800 g Dutch cream or other roasting potatoes, scrubbed and cut into wedges
- 185 g (1 cup) unpitted kalamata olives
- 1 tablespoon chopped parsley
- 150 g (1 cup) crumbled feta
- 1 teaspoon sea salt flakes

— Preheat the oven to 200°C (fan-forced).

— Use a small sharp knife to cut 10 evenly distributed small holes in the lamb. Into each hole, stuff 2–3 oregano leaves and ½ garlic clove; this should use up about half the oregano. Rub the olive oil over the lamb and generously season with salt and freshly ground black pepper.

— Place the lamb in a large roasting tin, transfer to the oven and roast for 25 minutes.

— Remove the roasting tin from the oven, pour in the wine and 190 ml (¾ cup) water, then cover the tin tightly with foil. Reduce the oven temperature to 140°C (fan-forced) and cook the lamb for a further 1 hour.

— Add the lemon, potatoes and olives to the roasting tin. Cover again with the foil and bake for a further 1¼ hours.

— Remove the foil, increase the oven temperature to 190°C (fan-forced), and leave to roast for a final 20 minutes.

— Remove the lamb from the roasting tin, cover loosely with foil and set aside to rest.

— Meanwhile, return the roasting tin to the oven, and roast the potatoes, uncovered, for an additional 20 minutes, so they start to brown.

— In a small bowl, mix together the parsley, feta and salt flakes.

— Transfer the lamb to a large serving dish and arrange the potatoes, olives and lemon quarters alongside. Separate the fat from the roasting tin juices, then drizzle the pan juices over the lamb. Sprinkle the feta mixture over the potatoes and serve.

PORK KNUCKLE WITH APPLE SAUCE & SAUERKRAUT

Serves 4

- 4 pork knuckles, preferably brined
- 2 onions, roughly chopped
- 2 carrots, roughly chopped
- 2 celery stalks, roughly chopped
- 4 dried bay leaves
- 20 black peppercorns
- 6 dried juniper berries
- 2 teaspoons salt, plus extra for sprinkling
- 200 g good-quality sauerkraut

BRINE (OPTIONAL)

- salt
- 5–6 dried juniper berries (optional)

— If you have been unable to buy brined knuckles, use the following method to prepare the knuckles 2 days ahead of time.

— Place the knuckles in a large container that will fit in your fridge, ensuring they can be completely submerged.

— To make the brine, measuring as you go, add enough cold water to completely submerge the knuckles. Based on how much water you've used, calculate how much salt you need — every 1 litre (4 cups) of water will need 155 g (½ cup) of salt. Transfer 600 ml of the water to a saucepan, then add the salt quantity that matches the entire amount of water, along with the juniper berries, if using. Bring to the boil, stirring well to dissolve the salt, then transfer to the fridge to cool completely. Pour the brine back into the container with the knuckles, then cover and leave for up to 2 days, checking now and then to ensure the knuckles stay submerged.

— When you're ready to start cooking, drain the knuckles and discard the brine. Using a pair of kitchen scissors, make 1 cm long cuts into the pork skin around the base of the knuckle, about 2 cm apart.

— If you don't have a stockpot large enough to fit all the pork knuckles together, divide the onion, carrot, celery, bay leaves, peppercorns, juniper berries and salt between two smaller saucepans, along with the knuckles. Otherwise, place them all in the one stockpot. Cover the knuckles with cold water.

— Bring to the boil, then reduce the heat to a simmer and cook for 1 hour. Test the knuckles by pushing a meat fork or a sharp knife into the pork — if the meat slides off easily, the knuckles are done. If there is still a little resistance, continue cooking for up to a further 30 minutes.

— Remove the knuckles from the liquid and set aside to cool slightly, then pat dry with paper towel. Strain the cooking liquid, reserving half the total liquid.

— Preheat the oven to 160°C (fan-forced).

— Use a sharp knife to score the skin around the knuckles. Rub a generous amount of salt into the skin — up to 1½ teaspoons per knuckle.

— Set a roasting rack in a roasting tin and place the knuckles on top. Pour 500 ml (2 cups) of the reserved cooking liquid into the roasting tin. Carefully transfer to the oven. Roast the knuckles for 1 hour, basting every now and then with the remaining reserved liquid.

— Use a meat thermometer to check that the internal temperature is above 70°C. If it isn't, roast the knuckles a little longer, checking every 15 minutes.

— Once the internal temperature has reached 70°C, carefully remove the liquid from the roasting tin.

— Return the knuckles to the oven and increase the oven temperature to 210°C (fan-forced). Roast for a further 30 minutes, or until the skin has turned into crisp crackling.

— Remove from the oven, cover loosely with foil and leave to rest for 20 minutes while you make the apple sauce.

— Place the apple in a small saucepan, along with the sugar, lemon juice and cinnamon, if using. Add 80 ml (⅓ cup) water and bring to the boil over medium heat. Reduce the heat to low, then cover and leave to cook for 15–20 minutes, or until the apple has completely broken down. Remove from the heat and mash with a fork, so that you have a chunky sauce.

— Gently heat the sauerkraut in a small saucepan until warmed through, then serve with the apple sauce and knuckles.

APPLE SAUCE

575 g granny smith apples, peeled, cored and diced

1½ tablespoons sugar

squeeze of lemon juice

pinch of ground cinnamon (optional)

SLOW-ROASTED RABBIT STEW

Serves 6

- 1 x 700 g rabbit
- 50 g (⅓ cup) plain flour
- 60 ml (¼ cup) olive oil
- 200 g pancetta, cut into batons
- 2 carrots, finely chopped
- 1 celery stalk, finely chopped
- 1 onion, finely chopped
- 2 garlic cloves, crushed
- 1 rosemary sprig
- 1 sage sprig
- 190 ml (¾ cup) red wine
- 400 g tin chopped tomatoes
- 375 ml (1½ cups) vegetable stock or water
- 2 roasted red capsicums, cut into strips
- 80 g (½ cup) cracked large green olives
- handful parsley

— Preheat the oven to 140°C (fan-forced). Rinse the rabbit and pat dry with paper towel. Chop the rabbit into pieces, as though you were cutting up a whole chicken: cut off the hind legs (which can also be cut in half again) and the front legs; cut the rib cage away and discard; cut the saddle into four pieces.

— Put the flour in a large zip-lock bag and season with salt and freshly ground black pepper. Add the rabbit pieces and shake to dust them in the flour. Shake off the excess flour.

— In a flameproof casserole dish with a tight-fitting lid, heat the olive oil over medium–high heat. Working in batches if necessary, sear the rabbit pieces all over for several minutes, or until golden. Transfer to a plate and set aside.

— Add the pancetta to the casserole dish and cook for 5 minutes, or until lightly browned. Reduce the heat to medium–low, add the carrot, celery and onion and cook, stirring occasionally, for 10 minutes, or until the vegetables are soft. Add the garlic and the herb sprigs and cook for 2–3 minutes, or until fragrant.

— Return the rabbit to the dish, add the wine and cook for 2 minutes, scraping the bottom of the dish to dislodge the lovely browned bits. Stir in the tomatoes and stock and bring to the boil.

— Put the lid on, transfer to the oven and bake for 1 hour. Stir in the capsicum, mixing well. Put the lid back on and bake for a further 30 minutes, or until the meat just begins to fall off the bones. Stir in the olives and parsley and serve.

CRISPY PORK BELLY WITH FIVE-SPICE & DIPPING SAUCE

Serves 4

- 1.2–1.4 kg piece of pork belly, skin on
- 1 teaspoon Chinese five-spice
- 1 tablespoon olive oil
- 1 tablespoon sea salt flakes
- 200 g rice stick noodles
- 2 short cucumbers, cut into thin batons
- shredded carrot, to serve
- coriander sprigs, to serve
- mint leaves, to serve
- lemon wedges, to serve

HOISIN & GINGER MARINADE

- 125 ml (½ cup) hoisin sauce
- 125 ml (½ cup) light soy sauce
- 1 tablespoon grated fresh ginger
- 1 tablespoon crushed garlic
- 125 ml (½ cup) shaoxing rice wine
- 1 tablespoon brown sugar

CHILLI GINGER DIPPING SAUCE

- 90 ml hoisin sauce
- 3 garlic cloves, crushed
- 45 ml light soy sauce
- 1 tablespoon grated fresh ginger
- 1 tablespoon honey
- 1 teaspoon chilli sauce

— Use a sharp knife to score the pork skin, if it hasn't been scored already by your butcher. Place the pork on a roasting rack in the sink, then pour a kettle of boiling water over the skin. Pat dry thoroughly.

— Mix the marinade ingredients together in a jug. Place the pork, skin side up, in a shallow dish large enough to lay it out flat. Being careful not to let it touch the skin, pour the marinade around the pork; the marinade is for the flesh only. Carefully transfer to the fridge and leave to dry, uncovered, for 2–3 hours, or overnight.

— When you're ready to start cooking, preheat the oven to 200°C (fan-forced).

— Remove the pork from the marinade and place in a roasting tin. Sprinkle the five-spice, olive oil and salt flakes over the skin and rub it all in, using your hands.

— Transfer to the oven and roast for 30 minutes to ensure a crispy crackling, then reduce the oven temperature to 150°C (fan-forced) and cook for a further 1 hour 20 minutes, or until the pork is tender. If the crackling isn't crisp enough at this point, place it under a hot grill for a few minutes.

— Remove from the oven, cover loosely with foil and leave to rest for 15 minutes.

— Just before serving, cook the noodles according to the packet instructions. Combine the dipping sauce ingredients in a small bowl, mixing well.

— Carve the pork and serve on a nest of noodles, topped with the cucumber, carrot and herbs, with the dipping sauce and lemon wedges alongside.

BOEUF EN CROUTE WITH RED WINE JUS

Serves 4–6

— To prepare the duxelles, put the dried porcini in a small bowl, cover with boiling water and leave to rehydrate for 15 minutes. Clean the fresh mushrooms, place in the large bowl of a food processor and blend until finely chopped. Set aside.

— Heat the butter in a frying pan over medium heat. Sauté the garlic and shallot for 3–4 minutes, or until translucent but not browned. Add the thyme sprigs and chopped fresh mushrooms and cook for about 6–8 minutes, until the mushrooms have darkened and released their juices into the pan.

— Drain the porcini, reserving 60 ml (¼ cup) of the soaking liquor. Finely chop the porcini and add to the pan with the white wine, then cook for 2–3 minutes. Add the porcini liquor, and leave the mushrooms to cook, stirring frequently, until all the liquid in the pan has disappeared, and you are left with a dark, fragrant, paste-like mixture. This process can take up to 20 minutes — be patient, as the elimination of water will be important for assembling the dish. Remove the thyme stems, stir in the parsley and set aside to cool completely.

— Remove the beef from the fridge and leave for 30 minutes to bring it to room temperature. Season well with salt and freshly ground black pepper.

— Heat the olive oil in a large frying pan over high heat. Sear the beef on all sides — including both ends — for about 2 minutes on each side. Remove to a plate and allow to cool slightly.

— Lay a large piece of plastic wrap, about 60 cm long, on a clean work surface. Lay 4–5 pieces of the prosciutto, slightly overlapping, on the plastic. Layer the remaining prosciutto at the base of the first row of slices, so that you end up with a 'sheet' of prosciutto large enough to completely encase the beef.

— Spread the duxelles evenly over the prosciutto layer, leaving at least 2 cm free on all edges. Place the beef on top. Using the end of the plastic wrap, roll the prosciutto tightly around the beef and duxelles.

- 1 x 750 g piece of beef fillet
- 2 tablespoons olive oil
- 8–10 slices prosciutto
- 375 g block or sheet of frozen butter puff pastry, thawed
- 1 free-range egg yolk, beaten
- sea salt flakes, for sprinkling

DUXELLES

- 10 g dried porcini mushrooms
- 400 g mixed fresh mushrooms
- 40 g butter
- 2 garlic cloves, crushed
- 1 French shallot, finely diced
- 2 large thyme sprigs
- 80 ml (⅓ cup) white wine
- 1 tablespoon chopped parsley

— Continue to wrap in the plastic, twisting the short edges, so that you end up with a tightly wrapped bundle, with the prosciutto completely encasing the beef and mushroom. Transfer to the fridge and leave to firm up for 10 minutes.

— Roll the pastry out to about 40 cm long, and 30 cm across, so that it will be large enough to completely encase the beef. Use the plastic-wrapped parcel to check the size before unwrapping the beef.

— Remove the plastic, then lay the prosciutto-wrapped bundle on the pastry. Tightly wrap the pastry around it, folding in the sides. Tightly wrap in another long length of plastic wrap, and return to the fridge again until ready to use; as long as it is well wrapped, the bundle can sit for several hours.

— Preheat the oven to 180°C (fan-forced).

— Decorate the pastry as you see fit, then brush with the beaten egg yolk and season with salt flakes. Place in a roasting tin and roast for 35 minutes for rare, or up to 45 minutes for medium-rare, until the pastry is golden brown. Remove from the oven and leave to rest for 10 minutes.

— While the beef is in the oven, make the red wine jus. Heat the olive oil over medium-high heat, add the garlic and shallot and cook for 3–4 minutes, stirring constantly. Increase the heat to high and add the thyme sprigs, bay leaf and red wine. Bring to the boil, reduce the heat and leave to simmer for 10 minutes, or until the wine has reduced by about two-thirds. Stir in the stock and continue to simmer for 10–15 minutes, or until the sauce has reduced and is starting to thicken. Strain, place back over medium heat and whisk in the butter to give a glossy finish.

— Serve the beef with the red wine jus in a gravy jug, for drizzling over.

RED WINE JUS

- 1 tablespoon olive oil
- 1 garlic clove, chopped
- 1 large French shallot, finely diced
- 3–4 thyme sprigs
- 1 bay leaf
- 400 ml red wine
- 350 ml beef stock
- 30 g butter, cubed

Boeuf en croute
with red wine jus

MINI LAMB ROASTS WITH CHIMICHURRI

Serves 4

— Preheat the oven to 200°C (fan-forced).

— Season the lamb well with salt and freshly ground black pepper. Place in a roasting tin and top with a drizzle of olive oil.

— Transfer to the oven and roast for 20 minutes for rare, 25–30 minutes for medium, or 35 minutes for well done.

— Remove from the oven, cover loosely with foil, and leave to rest for 10 minutes.

— While the lamb is resting, toss the tomatoes in a splash of olive oil, season with salt and pepper, place on a baking tray and roast for 10 minutes.

— Combine all the chimichurri ingredients in the bowl of a small food processor, and whiz until the herbs and onion are finely chopped.

— Carve the lamb and serve with the tomatoes and chimichurri.

2 mini lamb roasts, about 350 g each

olive oil, for drizzling

400 g cherry tomatoes, on the vine

CHIMICHURRI

60 g (2 cups, firmly packed) parsley

5–6 garlic cloves, roughly chopped

¼ red onion, roughly chopped

17 g (⅔ cup, firmly packed) fresh oregano leaves

80 ml (⅓ cup) red wine vinegar

¾ teaspoon chilli flakes

½ teaspoon salt

¼ teaspoon freshly ground black pepper

270 ml olive oil

ORIGINAL
LOUISIANA

STICKY ROAST PORK RIBS WITH SLAW

Serves 4

2 large racks of pork ribs, about 2 kg in total

DRY RUB

- 55 g (¼ cup, firmly packed) soft brown sugar
- ½ teaspoon salt
- 1 teaspoon cayenne pepper
- 2 tablespoons smoked paprika
- 1 tablespoon garlic powder
- 1 teaspoon mustard powder

BARBECUE SAUCE

- 230 g (1 cup, firmly packed) dark brown sugar
- 4 tablespoons smoked paprika
- 500 ml (2 cups) apple cider vinegar
- 250 ml (1 cup) tomato ketchup
- 90 ml worcestershire sauce
- 1 teaspoon liquid smoke (optional)

SLAW

- 200 g (2⅔ cups) shredded white cabbage
- 175 g (2⅓ cups) shredded red cabbage
- 1 large carrot, grated
- 4 spring onions, finely sliced
- 120 g whole-egg mayonnaise
- 60 g (¼ cup) sour cream
- 1 tablespoon lemon juice
- 1½ tablespoons pickled jalapeño chillies

— Preheat the oven to 130°C (fan-forced).

— Mix all the dry rub ingredients together in a small bowl. Using your hands, rub the spices well into the ribs, on all sides. Roll out two double layers of foil on a work surface, and wrap a rack of ribs in each. Crimp the top and sides of the foil so that the parcels are sealed, leaving a few centimetres between the foil and the meat.

— Place on a baking tray, transfer to the oven and bake for 2 hours.

— While the ribs are cooking, make the barbecue sauce and the slaw.

— For the barbecue sauce, place the sugar, paprika, vinegar, ketchup and worcestershire sauce in a small saucepan. Mix until combined, then bring to the boil. Reduce the heat and simmer for about 30 minutes, or until the sauce has reduced by half, and is thick and glossy. Stir in the liquid smoke, if using.

— For the slaw, combine all the cabbage, carrot and spring onion in a bowl. In a small bowl, mix together the mayonnaise, sour cream and lemon juice. Put the jalapeños on a chopping board and chop roughly, then use the back of a knife to mash them, so that you end up with a watery paste. Add to the mayonnaise mixture and stir well. Season to taste with salt and plenty of freshly ground black pepper. Toss through the slaw and set aside until ready to serve.

— When the 2 hours is up, remove the ribs from the oven and open the foil. Increase the oven temperature to 180°C (fan-forced). Liberally brush the ribs on all sides with the barbecue sauce, then return to the oven, meat side up, for 10 minutes.

— Remove from the oven and brush the meat side again generously with more barbecue sauce, then roast for a further 10 minutes.

— Serve the ribs with the slaw, with the remaining barbecue sauce on the side for drizzling and dipping.

BEEF POT ROAST

Serves 4–6

— Preheat the oven to 140°C (fan-forced).

— Heat the olive oil in a flameproof casserole dish over medium heat. Brown the beef well, for about 2 minutes on each side, then remove to a plate.

— Drain the fat from the casserole dish. Place the beef back in the dish, along with the wine, stock, thyme and rosemary sprigs. Put the lid on, transfer to the oven and cook for 1¼ hours, turning the beef over once during that time.

— Remove from the oven, add the potatoes and onions, put the lid back on and bake for 30 minutes.

— Add the carrots, then cover and bake for a further 30 minutes.

— Remove from the oven and allow the beef to rest for a few minutes before carving.

— Serve slices of the beef in bowls, along with the vegetables and a good ladleful of the broth. Enjoy with crusty bread.

- 60 ml (¼ cup) olive oil
- 1 x 1–1.4 kg piece of beef chuck or blade roast
- 250 ml (1 cup) white wine
- 500 ml (2 cups) beef stock
- 2 thyme sprigs
- 2 rosemary sprigs
- 8 new potatoes, scrubbed
- 8 baby onions, peeled
- 8–10 baby carrots, peeled and trimmed
- crusty bread, to serve

MUSTARD-GLAZED ROAST LEG OF HAM WITH PEACH SALSA

Serves 8–10

— Move an oven rack to the lowest rung, then preheat the oven to 140°C (fan-forced). Line a large roasting tin with foil or baking paper, and place a roasting rack in the tin.

— In a saucepan, combine the sugar, apple juice and maple syrup, stirring over medium heat until the sugar has dissolved. Remove from the heat and stir in the wholegrain and dijon mustards.

— Use a sharp knife to score the fat of the ham in a diamond pattern, taking care not to cut all the way through to the flesh. Stick a clove into the middle of each diamond, then place the ham on the roasting rack in the roasting tin. Baste all over with the maple syrup glaze.

— Transfer to the oven and roast for 15 minutes, then baste again with the glaze. Continue to roast for another 1¼ hours, basting at 20-minute intervals.

— When the ham is nearly ready, gently mix all the salsa ingredients together in a bowl.

— Remove the ham from the oven and serve with the peach salsa.

- 115 g (½ cup, firmly packed) soft brown sugar
- 125 ml (½ cup) apple juice
- 125 ml (½ cup) maple syrup
- 2 tablespoons wholegrain mustard
- 2 tablespoons dijon mustard
- 1 leg of ham, weighing 3–4 kg, skin removed
- whole cloves, to decorate

PEACH SALSA

- 4 peaches, peeled and diced
- grated zest and juice of 1 lime
- 1 fresh jalapeño chilli, seeded and finely diced
- ½ red onion, diced or finely sliced
- 3 tablespoons chopped coriander leaves
- 2 tomatoes, diced
- 1 red capsicum, finely diced

ROAST BEEF RIBS WITH PARSNIPS & HORSERADISH CREAM

Serves 6

2 onions

2 carrots

3–4 parsnips

2.3–2.5 kg rack of beef ribs (3–4 'points' or bones)

HERB & SALT CRUST

1 tablespoon black peppercorns

2 teaspoons rock salt

1 teaspoon garlic salt

1 tablespoon chopped parsley

1 tablespoon chopped rosemary

60 ml (¼ cup) olive oil

HORSERADISH CREAM

60 g (¼ cup) prepared horseradish (from a jar)

125 ml (½ cup) thickened cream, whipped

90 g (⅓ cup) sour cream

1 teaspoon chopped chives (optional)

— Preheat the oven to 200°C (fan-forced).

— For the herb and salt crust, use a mortar and pestle to roughly bash the peppercorns and rock salt for a few seconds, so they are broken down slightly, but still quite coarse. Transfer to a small bowl and add the garlic salt, parsley, rosemary and olive oil, stirring to combine.

— Peel the onions, carrots and parsnips. Roughly chop the onions and carrots and arrange them around a roasting tin. Place the beef ribs on the vegetables, bone side down. Rub the salt crust mixture onto the beef, making sure all sides are well coated. Add the parsnips around the beef.

— Transfer to the oven and roast for 15 minutes. Reduce the oven temperature to 160°C (fan-forced), and continue to roast to your preferred doneness — for rare, 15 minutes per 450 g; for medium, 20 minutes per 450 g; for well done, 25 minutes per 450 g. Use a meat thermometer if in doubt — 60°C for rare, 65–70°C for medium, and 70–75°C for well done.

— Transfer the beef and parsnips to a plate, cover loosely with foil and a tea towel, and leave to rest for 20 minutes, while you make the horseradish cream.

— Combine the horseradish cream ingredients in a bowl. Season to taste with salt and freshly ground black pepper, mixing well.

— Carve the beef and serve with the parsnips and horseradish cream. Yorkshire puddings (see page 121) are a wonderful accompaniment.

LAMB SHANKS WITH CANNELLINI BEANS

Serves 4

— Preheat the oven to 140°C (fan-forced).

— Put the flour in a large zip-lock bag and season well with salt and freshly ground black pepper. Toss the lamb shanks, one at a time, in the bag, until evenly coated with flour. Set aside.

— Heat the olive oil in a flameproof casserole dish over medium heat. Working with two at a time, brown the shanks well for about 2 minutes on each side, then remove to a plate.

— Add the onion, garlic and chorizo to the casserole dish and fry for 4–5 minutes, or until softened. Add the rosemary, paprika, ale, stock and tomatoes, stirring well. Season with more salt and pepper, bring to the boil, then remove from the heat.

— Return the shanks to the dish, put the lid on and transfer to the oven. Cook for 1½ hours, turning the shanks once.

— Stir in the beans and cook for a further 20 minutes.

— To make the salad, toss the spinach and red onion together, then drizzle with the olive oil and vinegar and toss again.

— Serve the shanks with the salad.

2 tablespoons plain flour

4 lamb shanks

2 tablespoons olive oil

2 onions, diced

3 garlic cloves, crushed

1 chorizo sausage, diced

2 rosemary sprigs

1 tablespoon smoked paprika

250 ml (1 cup) pale ale

250 ml (1 cup) beef stock

600 g chopped tinned tomatoes

2 x 400 g tins cannellini beans, drained and rinsed

BABY SPINACH SALAD

200 g baby spinach

¼ red onion, finely sliced

3 teaspoons olive oil

1 teaspoon balsamic vinegar

05

SIDES

THYME & SUMAC HASSELBACK POTATOES
p.118

YORKSHIRE PUDDINGS
p.121

MAPLE ROASTED PUMPKIN
p.122

BACON-WRAPPED STUFFED ONIONS
p.125

ASPARAGUS BUNDLES WRAPPED IN PROSCIUTTO
p.126

JALAPEÑO THREE-CHEESE CAULIFLOWER
p.129

ROASTED RED CABBAGE WITH DRIED FIG GLAZE
p.130

LEMON & ROSEMARY SMASHED CANNELLINI BEANS
p.133

ROAST SMASHED POTATOES
p.134

BRUSSELS SPROUTS WITH CANNELLINI BEANS & CRUMBLED PANCETTA
p.137

CAULIFLOWER & CELERIAC MASH WITH SAGE BURNT BUTTER
p.138

NEW POTATO SALAD WITH FRESH HERBS & CRISP CAPERS
p.141

MEDITERRANEAN TRAY BAKE
p.142

BARBECUED CORN SALAD WITH CHIPOTLE MAYO
p.145

COLCANNON
p.146

ROASTED BROCCOLI SALAD WITH PICKLED ONION
p.149

ORANGE & THYME ROASTED BABY CARROTS
p.150

THYME & SUMAC HASSELBACK POTATOES

Serves 4

- 8 medium-sized roasting potatoes
- 60 g butter
- 2 tablespoons olive oil
- 1 teaspoon thyme leaves, plus extra to garnish
- 1 teaspoon chopped rosemary leaves
- 1 teaspoon sumac

— Preheat the oven to 180°C (fan-forced). Line a baking tray with foil.

— Lay one potato on a chopping board, and place two wooden spoons or two large chopsticks along the length of either side of the potato. Starting at one end and working to the other, cut slices into the potato, about 2–3 mm apart, bringing the knife down to the wooden spoons, which will prevent you cutting all the way through. This will take some time, but the effect will be worth your patience. Repeat with the remaining potatoes.

— Gently fan out the potatoes, to allow the fat to get between the slices, then place on the baking tray.

— Melt about 1 tablespoon of the butter, and mix with the olive oil, thyme, rosemary and sumac. Brush the butter mixture onto the potatoes, using the bristles to gently get some of the butter between the slices. Season with salt and freshly ground black pepper.

— Transfer to the oven and roast for 30 minutes. Melt the remaining butter, use it to baste the potatoes, then roast for a further 15 minutes.

— Season with salt and pepper, garnish with extra thyme and serve.

YORKSHIRE PUDDINGS

Makes 12

— Move an oven rack to the upper shelf, then preheat the oven to 210°C (fan-forced).

— Drizzle the dripping into the cups of a 12-hole muffin tin, dividing it equally. Transfer to the oven and leave to heat for 10 minutes, or until smoking.

— Meanwhile, mix together the remaining ingredients in a bowl until you have a smooth batter. Set aside until the dripping has heated.

— Carefully remove the muffin tin from the oven. Working carefully, as the fat will be very hot, divide the batter among the 12 muffin holes.

— Place back in the oven and bake for 25–30 minutes, without opening the oven, until the puddings are golden brown and puffed up. Serve immediately.

- 80 ml (⅓ cup) beef dripping or sunflower oil
- 250 g (1⅔ cups) plain flour
- 200 ml full-cream milk
- 110 ml cold water
- 4 free-range eggs, beaten
- pinch of salt

MAPLE-ROASTED PUMPKIN

Serves 4

60 ml (¼ cup) olive oil

1 butternut pumpkin

60 ml (¼ cup) maple syrup

50 g (½ cup) pecans, chopped

— Preheat the oven to 160°C (fan-forced). Pour half the olive oil into a roasting tin and place it in the oven to heat up.

— Peel the pumpkin and slice into rounds, 2 cm thick. Cut the slices in half and remove the seeds and stringy flesh.

— Remove the roasting tin from the oven and carefully add the pumpkin in a single layer. Season with salt and freshly ground black pepper and return to the oven for 10–15 minutes, turning occasionally.

— Meanwhile, combine the remaining olive oil and the maple syrup in a small screw-top jar. Season with salt and freshly ground black pepper and add the chopped pecans. Pop the lid on and give the jar a good shake.

— Pour the dressing over the pumpkin in the tin and roast for a further 10–15 minutes, turning occasionally to stop the dressing sticking to the base of the tin, until the pumpkin is soft and cooked through and the pecans are caramelised.

— Transfer to a serving dish and serve immediately.

BACON-WRAPPED STUFFED ONIONS

Makes 6

- 6 medium sized onions
- 1 tablespoon olive oil
- 2 pork sausages, removed from their casings and chopped
- 1 celery stalk, finely sliced
- 1½ teaspoons thyme leaves
- 1½ teaspoons chopped sage
- 100 g (1¼ cups) fresh breadcrumbs
- 20 g butter, melted
- 80 ml (⅓ cup) chicken stock
- 6 slices streaky bacon

— Preheat the oven to 180°C (fan-forced).

— Cut the tops and bottoms from the onions, so that they sit flat on a chopping board, then peel them. Working with one onion at a time, make a perpendicular slit through the first two outer layers of the onion. Use your fingers to gently prise the layers open, enough so that the inner layers of the onion can be pushed out, leaving you with a hollow round. Dice the inner layers of two of the onions, and set aside; save the remaining onion inners for another use.

— Place the hollowed-out onions in a bowl of cold water and leave to soak while you make the stuffing.

— Heat the olive oil in a frying pan and fry the sausage meat over medium heat until cooked through, mashing with a wooden spoon as it cooks to ensure there are no large pieces of meat. Remove from the pan with a slotted spoon, into a bowl.

— Add the diced onion and celery to the pan. Reduce the heat to medium–low and cook for 4–5 minutes, or until softened, but not browned.

— Add the onion and celery to the sausage meat, along with the herbs and breadcrumbs. Season well with salt and freshly ground black pepper. Add the melted butter and stock, then stir to combine.

— Drain the onions. Lay one on a flat surface, and use your hands or a small spoon to stuff the onion cavity with the sausage mixture until full, ensuring the stuffing is firmly packed. Wrap a slice of bacon around the onion, then secure with a toothpick. Repeat with the remaining onions, stuffing mixture and bacon.

— Transfer to the oven and roast for 20 minutes, or until the bacon is golden brown.

— Serve hot, removing the toothpicks just before serving.

ASPARAGUS BUNDLES WRAPPED IN PROSCIUTTO

Serves 4

- 2 tablespoons lemon juice
- 2 teaspoons dijon mustard
- 75 ml olive oil
- 20–24 asparagus spears
- 4 slices prosciutto
- small handful shaved parmesan

— Preheat the oven to 180°C (fan-forced). Line a baking tray with baking paper.

— To make the dressing, whisk together the lemon juice, mustard and 60 ml (¼ cup) of the olive oil. Season with salt and freshly ground black pepper and set aside.

— Trim the woody ends from the asparagus, and toss the spears with the remaining olive oil, massaging the oil in to ensure each spear is coated. Season with salt and pepper.

— Arrange the asparagus into four bundles, with 5–6 spears in each. Tightly wrap a slice of prosciutto around each bundle, and place on the baking tray, seam side down.

— Transfer to the oven and roast for 10–12 minutes, or until the prosciutto begins to crisp and the spears are just tender.

— Transfer to a serving dish, drizzle some dressing over each bundle, top with the parmesan and serve.

JALAPEÑO THREE-CHEESE CAULIFLOWER

Serves 4–6

1 cauliflower, stalk removed, cut into large florets
75 g butter
75 g (½ cup) plain flour
560 ml (2¼ cups) full-cream milk
65 g cheddar, grated
65 g red leicester, grated
65 g mozzarella, grated
3 tablespoons chopped pickled jalapeño chillies
60 g (¾ cup) fresh breadcrumbs

— Preheat the oven to 160°C (fan-forced).

— Cook the cauliflower florets in a large saucepan of salted boiling water, until almost tender when tested with a sharp knife. Drain and set aside.

— To make the cheese sauce, melt 45 g of the butter in a saucepan over medium heat. Add the flour and cook, stirring, for 3–4 minutes. Using a spoon or whisk, stir in about 170 ml (⅔ cup) of the milk, ensuring there are no lumps. When fully combined, stir in the rest of the milk. Bring to the boil, reduce the heat to low and simmer for 2–3 minutes.

— Add 50 g of the cheddar, 50 g of the red leicester, and 50 g of the mozzarella. Stir well to combine, until all the cheese has melted and the sauce has thickened. Remove from the heat and stir in the jalapeño chillies.

— Arrange the cauliflower in a baking dish in a single layer, then pour the cheese sauce over.

— Combine the breadcrumbs and remaining cheese in a bowl. Melt the remaining butter, drizzle over the breadcrumb mixture and mix well. Scatter the mixture over the cauliflower.

— Transfer to the oven and bake for 40 minutes, or until the topping is golden and the cheese sauce is bubbling. Remove from the oven and serve.

ROASTED RED CABBAGE WITH DRIED FIG GLAZE

Serves 4–6

- 100 g dried figs, finely chopped
- 2 tablespoons red wine vinegar
- 125 ml (½ cup) Pedro Ximénez, or any good-quality sweet Spanish sherry
- a few rosemary sprigs, leaves picked
- ½ red cabbage, chopped into 4–6 wedges
- 2 garlic cloves, finely chopped
- 125 ml (½ cup) olive oil

— To make the glaze, combine the figs, vinegar, sherry, rosemary and 60 ml (¼ cup) water in a small saucepan, then season with salt and freshly ground black pepper. Cook over medium heat for 10–12 minutes, or until the liquid has reduced to a syrup. Set aside.

— Meanwhile, preheat the oven to 160°C (fan-forced). Line a large baking tray with foil.

— Place the cabbage wedges on the baking tray. Sprinkle with the garlic, drizzle with the olive oil and season with salt and pepper. Roast for 10–15 minutes, or until the edges are starting to crisp.

— Turn the cabbage wedges over and spoon the fig glaze over. Return to the oven and roast for a further 10–15 minutes, or until the cabbage is cooked through and the glaze is bubbling. Serve warm.

LEMON & ROSEMARY SMASHED CANNELLINI BEANS

Serves 4

— Heat the olive oil in a saucepan over medium heat. Add the onion and garlic and fry gently for 3–4 minutes, or until the onion is soft and translucent, but not browned.

— Add the beans and stock and bring to the boil. Simmer for 3–4 minutes, or until the beans are fully warmed through.

— Remove from the heat and add the crème fraîche, lemon juice and rosemary. Use a potato masher to mash the beans, until they are semi-smooth.

— Serve warm, garnished with lemon zest and extra rosemary.

- 1 tablespoon olive oil
- 1 onion, finely diced
- 2 garlic cloves, crushed
- 2 x 400 g tins cannellini beans, drained and rinsed
- 60 ml (¼ cup) chicken stock
- 2 tablespoons crème fraîche
- 1 tablespoon lemon juice
- lemon zest, to garnish
- ¾ teaspoon finely chopped rosemary, plus extra to garnish

ROAST SMASHED POTATOES

Serves 4

1 kg Dutch cream or other roasting potatoes, peeled and cut into evenly sized chunks

3 tablespoons duck fat

2 rosemary sprigs

8 garlic cloves, unpeeled

sea salt flakes, for sprinkling

— Preheat the oven to 180°C (fan-forced).

— Bring the potatoes to the boil in a saucepan of salted water. Reduce the heat and leave to simmer for 5–6 minutes. Drain in a colander, and return to the saucepan. Leave for 5 minutes to allow the excess moisture to evaporate, then cover the pan and violently shake, so that the edges of the potatoes get roughed up.

— Put the duck fat in a large roasting tin, transfer to the oven and leave for 5 minutes to heat up. Carefully remove from the oven and add the potatoes, taking care as the hot fat may splatter.

— Toss the potatoes to ensure they are evenly coated in the fat, then return to the oven. Roast for 30 minutes, untouched.

— Remove the roasting tin from the oven. Turn the potatoes over, gently pressing down on each using a potato masher, to squish them slightly. Add the rosemary and garlic and roast for a further 20–30 minutes, or until the potato edges are crispy and golden brown.

— Serve hot, topped with the roasted garlic and rosemary sprigs, and sprinkled with plenty of sea salt flakes.

BRUSSELS SPROUTS WITH CANNELLINI BEANS & CRUMBLED PANCETTA

Serves 4

- 100 g sliced pancetta
- 300 g brussels sprouts, trimmed and cut in half
- 1 tablespoon olive oil
- 30 g butter, cubed
- 400 g tin cannellini beans, drained and rinsed
- 125 ml (½ cup) chicken stock
- 2 tablespoons grated parmesan
- 1 lemon, quartered

— Preheat the oven to 180°C (fan-forced). Line a baking tray with baking paper.

— Place the pancetta on the baking paper and roast for 4–5 minutes, or until crisp. Remove from the oven, leave to cool, then break into pieces. Set aside and keep warm.

— Remove the baking paper, then arrange the brussels sprouts on the baking tray. Add the olive oil, season with salt and freshly ground black pepper and toss well. Dot the cubed butter over the sprouts, then roast for 15–20 minutes, or until slightly charred, turning them over halfway through.

— While the sprouts are in the oven, put the beans in a small saucepan with the stock over low heat. Bring to the boil, then simmer gently for 10 minutes, or until warmed through.

— Using a slotted spoon, remove the beans from the stock and put them into a serving dish. Toss with the parmesan. Scatter the brussels sprouts over then crumble the pancetta over the top. Serve warm, with the lemon wedges for squeezing over.

CAULIFLOWER & CELERIAC MASH WITH SAGE BURNT BUTTER

Serves 4

750 g cauliflower, cut into florets

375 g celeriac, peeled and diced

75 g crème fraîche or sour cream

75 g butter

8–10 sage leaves

— Place the cauliflower and celeriac in a saucepan of boiling water. Bring to the boil, then reduce the heat and simmer for 15 minutes, or until the vegetables are tender. Drain.

— Transfer the vegetables to a food processor and blend for a few seconds, until mostly smooth — a few lumps are okay.

— Mix in the crème fraîche, then season with salt and freshly ground black pepper. Transfer to a serving dish and keep warm.

— Melt the butter in a small saucepan over medium heat and add the sage leaves. Continue to cook until the sage is crispy and the butter is foaming and a nut-brown colour.

— Pour the mixture over the mash and serve immediately.

NEW POTATO SALAD WITH FRESH HERBS & CRISP CAPERS

Serves 4–6

- 1 kg new potatoes
- 90 ml olive oil, plus extra for deep-frying
- 2 tablespoons red wine vinegar
- 2 teaspoons wholegrain mustard
- 2 teaspoons dijon mustard
- 2 tablespoons capers
- 2 tablespoons chopped chives
- 2 tablespoons chopped parsley
- 1 tablespoon chopped basil
- 30 g (1 cup, firmly packed) watercress sprigs

— Place the potatoes in a large saucepan of cold water. Bring to the boil, then reduce the heat and simmer for 15 minutes, or until cooked through. Drain and set aside.

— Meanwhile, pour the 90 ml olive oil into a small bowl. Whisk in the vinegar and both the mustards, then set aside.

— Drain the capers and pat dry using paper towel.

— Heat about 1 cm olive oil in a small saucepan over medium–high heat, until a cube of bread turns brown in 10 seconds after being dropped in. Carefully lower the capers into the oil, standing back as they may spatter. Cook for 30 seconds, until the capers open out. Remove using a slotted spoon and drain on paper towel.

— Cut the warm potatoes in half, or into slices if they are larger. Combine in a bowl with the herbs, watercress and vinegar dressing. Season to taste with salt and freshly ground black pepper, then scatter the capers over and serve.

— This salad is also delicious cold, although the fried capers are best served warm.

MEDITERRANEAN TRAY BAKE

Serves 6

- 10 thyme sprigs
- 10 rosemary sprigs, leaves picked
- 5 garlic cloves, peeled and smashed
- 250 ml (1 cup) olive oil
- 6–8 baby carrots
- 2 fennel bulbs, sliced
- 1 large or 2 small eggplants, chopped
- 1 zucchini, chopped
- 2 red onions, each cut into 8 wedges
- 2 capsicums, cut into wedges
- 6 baby truss tomatoes
- 150 g black olives
- 2 lemons, cut in half
- 100 g ricotta

— Combine the herbs, garlic and olive oil in a screw-top jar and shake thoroughly to combine. Set aside to infuse for 10 minutes.

— Set an oven rack near the top of the oven, then preheat the oven to 215°C (fan-forced).

— Arrange the carrots, fennel, eggplant, zucchini and onion in one very large roasting tin, or two smaller ones, spreading them out in a single layer, to stop them becoming soft and leaching too much liquid. Drizzle with the herbed oil mixture, then roast in the oven for 20 minutes, turning the vegetables halfway through.

— Add the capsicum, tomatoes, olives and lemon halves, and gently toss to coat them in the oil. Roast for a further 20 minutes, or until the vegetables are cooked through and starting to crisp.

— Transfer to a large serving platter and scatter the ricotta over. This wonderful roasted vegetable assortment pairs brilliantly with grilled meats and fish.

BARBECUED CORN SALAD WITH CHIPOTLE MAYO

Serves 4

- 1 tablespoon olive oil
- 3 corn cobs, husks and silks removed
- 75 g (¼ cup) mayonnaise, preferably Kewpie
- 1¼ teaspoons chipotle sauce
- 3 spring onions, finely sliced
- 1 tablespoon chopped coriander leaves
- 1 lime, zested, then cut into cheeks

— Preheat a barbecue to medium–high. Brush the olive oil over the corn cobs, then place on the hot barbecue and cook for 10–15 minutes, or until the corn is cooked through, turning evenly throughout cooking so there are nice dark char marks on all sides. Remove from the barbecue and set aside until cool enough to handle.

— In a small bowl, mix together the mayonnaise and chipotle sauce.

— Cut the kernels from the cobs and place in a flat serving dish. Season with salt and freshly ground black pepper. Dot the chipotle mayo around the dish, then scatter over the spring onions and coriander.

— Finish with the lime zest and serve the cheeks on the side.

COLCANNON

Serves 4

- 1 kg Dutch cream or other mashing potatoes, peeled
- 1 tablespoon olive oil
- 60 g butter
- 200 g smoked bacon, finely sliced
- 225 g (3 cups) shredded white or savoy cabbage
- 3 tablespoons chopped chives

— Place the potatoes in a large saucepan, cover with plenty of cold water and add a large pinch of salt. Bring to the boil, then reduce the heat and simmer for 15 minutes, or until tender.

— Meanwhile, heat the olive oil and 1 tablespoon of the butter in a large frying pan over medium–high heat. Add the bacon and cook for 2–3 minutes, then add the cabbage and stir to combine. Cook for a further 5–6 minutes, or until the cabbage has wilted and the bacon is crispy.

— When the potatoes are ready, drain them, then pass them through a potato ricer, back into the pan. Add the chives, remaining butter, and the sautéed cabbage and bacon mixture. Season with salt and pepper, mix well to combine, and serve immediately.

ROASTED BROCCOLI SALAD WITH PICKLED ONION

Serves 4

500 g broccoli
2 tablespoons olive oil
50 g (½ cup) pecans, toasted
40 g (⅓ cup) dried cranberries
80 g goat's cheese, crumbled

QUICK PICKLED ONION

60 ml (¼ cup) white wine vinegar
2 tablespoons sugar
1 red onion, finely sliced

LEMON, HERB & CAPER DRESSING

1 tablespoon chopped capers
juice of ½ lemon
2 tablespoons olive oil
½ teaspoon caster sugar
2 tablespoons chopped mint
2 tablespoons chopped parsley

— To pickle the onion, place the vinegar and sugar in a heatproof bowl and stir. Add the onion, then pour in 125 ml (½ cup) boiling water and leave to sit for 20 minutes.

— Preheat the oven to 200°C (fan-forced).

— Blanch the broccoli in a saucepan of salted boiling water for 3 minutes, then refresh under cold water and drain well.

— Cut the broccoli into bite-sized florets and transfer to a baking tray. Drizzle all over with the olive oil and season with salt and freshly ground black pepper.

— Transfer to the oven and roast for 15–20 minutes, turning the broccoli halfway through. Remove from the oven and keep warm.

— To make the dressing, mix together the capers, lemon juice, olive oil and sugar. Add the mint and parsley, stirring to combine.

— Drain the pickled onion, discarding the liquid.

— Arrange the warm broccoli on a flat serving plate, then scatter over the pecans, cranberries, goat's cheese and pickled onion. Drizzle with the dressing and serve warm.

ORANGE & THYME ROASTED BABY CARROTS

Serves 4

- 500 g baby carrots, scrubbed
- 30 g butter
- juice of ½ orange, plus the zest cut into long strips using a vegetable peeler
- 3–4 thyme sprigs, plus extra to garnish
- 2 tablespoons honey
- sea salt flakes, for sprinkling

— Preheat the oven to 180°C (fan-forced).

— Place the carrots, butter, orange juice, orange zest strips and thyme in a roasting tin large enough to fit the carrots in a single layer. Cover the roasting tin tightly with a double layer of foil.

— Transfer to the oven and roast for 20 minutes.

— Remove the roasting tin from the oven, and take off the foil. Drizzle the honey over the carrots.

— Increase the oven temperature to 210°C (fan-forced). Roast the carrots for a further 10–15 minutes, checking once or twice, until the edges start to caramelise.

— Transfer to a serving dish. Garnish with extra thyme, season with sea salt flakes and freshly ground black pepper and serve.

06

DESSERTS

ROASTED BERRIES WITH ALMOND CRUMBLE & ROSEWATER CREAM
p.154

APPLE & BLUEBERRY PIE
p.157

ROASTED WHITE CHOCOLATE DIP WITH GRISSINI
p.158

ROAST FIGS WITH VANILLA MASCARPONE
p.161

CINNAMON-ROASTED PEACHES WITH FRESH RICOTTA, THYME & HONEYED HAZELNUTS
p.162

ROAST MACADAMIA DARK CHOCOLATE BROWNIES
p.165

BAKED LEMON CHEESECAKE WITH RASPBERRY GLAZE
p.166

PEACH & BLUEBERRY COBBLER
p.169

ROAST BANANA ICE CREAM WITH SALTED CARAMEL PECANS
p.170

ROAST CHERRY BAKEWELL TART
p.173

ROASTED BERRIES WITH ALMOND CRUMBLE & ROSEWATER CREAM

Serves 4

250 g (1⅔ cups) strawberries, hulled and halved

150 g fresh blackberries

2 tablespoons rosewater

150 ml cream

small handful mint, to garnish

ALMOND CRUMBLE

75 g (½ cup) plain flour

115 g (½ cup) caster sugar

60 g butter, chopped

45 g (½ cup) flaked almonds

— Put the strawberries and blackberries in a small bowl, drizzle with 1 tablespoon of the rosewater and leave to sit for 30 minutes.

— Whip the cream, mix the remaining rosewater through and set aside in the fridge until ready to serve.

— Preheat the oven to 160°C (fan-forced). Line two baking trays with baking paper.

— To make the crumble, combine the flour, sugar, butter and a pinch of salt in the bowl of a small food processor and pulse until the mixture resembles fine breadcrumbs. Transfer to one of the baking trays and bake for 10 minutes.

— Remove the crumble mixture from the oven and add the almonds. Transfer the berry mixture to the other baking tray.

— Place both trays in the oven and bake for a further 10–15 minutes, or until the crumble mixture is golden brown, and the berries are softened and lightly roasted.

— If any of the crumble edges are looking a bit too brown, remove and discard them.

— Divide the warm fruit and crumble among four bowls. Top each with a dollop of the rosewater cream and garnish with mint leaves.

APPLE & BLUEBERRY PIE

Serves 8–10

— Grease a 22 cm loose-based tart tin with butter.

— To make the pastry, pulse the flour, salt and butter in a food processor until the mixture resembles breadcrumbs. Slowly add the water, until the mixture comes together.

— Turn out onto a clean work surface and gently knead into a ball. Wrap in plastic wrap and rest the pastry in the fridge for at least 30 minutes.

— Put the blueberries, sugar, cornflour and cinnamon in a bowl. Mix together, mashing with a fork three or four times so that a few of the blueberries break. Leave to sit until the dough has finished resting.

— Preheat the oven to 180°C (fan-forced).

— Divide the dough into two equal portions. Roll out one piece to 3 mm thick, then carefully line the tart tin, leaving any excess overlapping the sides. Roll out the second piece of pastry to the same size, then cut it into ten strips, about 2 cm wide.

— Arrange the apple slices evenly over the pastry base. Evenly spoon the blueberry mixture over the apples, then dot the butter over the blueberries.

— To make the lattice top, arrange five of the pastry strips evenly on top of the filling, then bend the 2nd and 4th strips up to about halfway back. Lay one strip perpendicular to the others where the bend occurs. Unfold the 2nd and 4th strips, then fold back the 1st, 3rd and 5th strips (i.e., the ones you hadn't folded before). Lay another strip perpendicular at the fold, 1–1.5 cm below from the last strip, then unfold the 1st, 3rd and 5th strips. Turn back the 2nd and 4th strips again, lay another strip perpendicular at the fold, 1–1.5 cm below from the last strip, then unfold.

— Repeat the process on the upper side of the pie, until you have a full lattice. Use a small sharp knife to trim the excess pastry from the edges. Crimp the edges together using a fork, or your thumb and forefinger.

— Brush the lattice with the beaten egg, and sprinkle with sugar. Transfer to the lower rack of the oven and bake for 30–40 minutes, or until the pastry is golden brown. Cut into slices to serve. This pie is also delicious cold.

40 g butter, plus extra for greasing

350 g (2¼ cups) fresh blueberries

75 g (⅓ cup) sugar, plus extra for sprinkling

2 tablespoons cornflour

½ teaspoon ground cinnamon

3 large granny smith apples, peeled, cored and roughly sliced

1 free-range egg, beaten

PASTRY

460 g plain flour

¾ teaspoon salt

315 g butter, cubed and chilled

30 ml iced water, approximately

ROASTED WHITE CHOCOLATE DIP WITH GRISSINI

Serves 6

— Preheat the oven to 120°C (fan-forced). Line a baking tray with foil

— Scatter the chocolate on the baking tray and roast for 10 minutes. Remove from the oven and stir the chocolate with a spatula, mixing the browned chocolate on the bottom with the paler chocolate on top. Spread the chocolate out with a palette knife and pop back in the oven.

— Repeat this process every 5–10 minutes, until the chocolate is a deep golden colour. Don't worry too much if your chocolate turns grainy instead of melted, as it will later be blitzed in a food processor.

— Set the chocolate aside to cool completely. Turn the oven off at this point, as the grissini dough will need to prove for 2 hours.

— To make the grissini, combine the water, yeast and sugar in a small jug and set aside for 10 minutes, or until bubbles appear on the surface.

— Place the flour and salt in a large bowl and make a well in the centre. Pour in the olive oil and yeast mixture and bring together with your hands until you have a rough dough. Knead on a lightly floured surface for 10 minutes, or until the dough is smooth and silky. Transfer to an oiled bowl, cover with a tea towel and set aside in a warm place to prove for 1 hour.

— Roll the dough out into a large rectangle, about 1 cm thick. Cover with a tea towel and leave to prove in a warm place for a further 1 hour.

— Preheat the oven to 160°C (fan-forced). Sprinkle sea salt flakes over the dough and gently run a rolling pin over the top. Cut the dough into 1 cm thick lengths, then cut the lengths in half. Gently pull and twist each piece of dough into a stick shape. Transfer to a baking tray and bake for 20 minutes, or until light brown and crisp. Set aside to cool.

— Transfer the cooled roasted white chocolate to a food processor and sprinkle with sea salt flakes. Add the crème fraîche and process until you have a smooth, thick sauce; you may need to add an extra few teaspoons of crème fraîche to get the consistency just right. Transfer to a serving bowl and serve with the grissini for dipping.

200 g white chocolate (at least 30% cocoa butter), broken into pieces

pinch of sea salt flakes

1 tablespoon crème fraîche, approximately

GRISSINI

150 ml lukewarm water

2 teaspoons active dried yeast

1 teaspoon sugar

300 g (2 cups) bread flour, plus extra for dusting

1 teaspoon salt

2 tablespoons olive oil, plus extra for greasing

sea salt flakes

ROAST FIGS WITH VANILLA MASCARPONE

Serves 4

— Preheat the oven to 200°C (fan-forced). Line a roasting tin with baking paper.

— Cut the stems off the figs. Sit the figs upright in the roasting tin, then slice a deep cross in the top of each fig, nearly all the way through, but not quite — you just want the figs to open out a little to hold the sauce.

— Melt the butter in a small saucepan. Remove from the heat and stir in the brown sugar and sherry until the sugar has dissolved. Spoon the sauce over the figs.

— Transfer to the oven and roast for 10–12 minutes, or until the figs have fanned out into 'flowers' and look soft and caramelised.

— Meanwhile, combine the mascarpone, icing sugar and vanilla seeds in a small bowl and whisk well until smooth and light.

— Place two figs on each serving plate and drizzle with any sauce from the roasting tin. Scatter over the pistachios and serve with a dollop of the vanilla mascarpone.

- 8 large fresh figs
- 100 g butter
- 55 g (¼ cup, firmly packed) soft brown sugar
- 2 tablespoons Pedro Ximénez, or any good quality sweet Spanish sherry
- 250 g mascarpone
- 3 tablespoons icing sugar
- 1 vanilla bean, split lengthways and seeds removed
- handful pistachios, roughly chopped

CINNAMON-ROASTED PEACHES WITH FRESH RICOTTA, THYME & HONEYED HAZELNUTS

Serves 4

- 70 g (½ cup) hazelnuts, roasted and peeled
- 2 tablespoons honey
- 3 tablespoons brown sugar, approximately
- 80 g butter, cut into 8 pieces
- ¼ teaspoon ground cinnamon
- 1 teaspoon thyme leaves
- 4 peaches, cut in half, stones removed
- 100 g fresh ricotta

— Preheat the oven to 180°C (fan-forced). Line two baking trays with baking paper.

— Put the hazelnuts in a non-stick frying pan over medium heat. Add the honey and leave for 2–3 minutes, swirling occasionally so that the honey melts and covers the nuts. Transfer to one of the baking trays, separating the nuts as you go. Leave to cool, then chop roughly and set aside.

— On the second baking tray, pile the sugar into eight separate little mounds, using about 1½ teaspoons of sugar for each mound, and leaving enough space in between for the peaches to sit on top.

— Top each little sugar mound with a piece of butter, then sprinkle with the cinnamon. Divide half the thyme leaves among the mounds, then place half a peach, cut side down, onto each mound.

— Transfer to the oven and roast for 15–20 minutes, or until the peaches are soft and the sugar has dissolved.

— Divide the warm peach halves among four plates. Divide the ricotta between them, then scatter over the honeyed hazelnuts and remaining thyme leaves. Serve warm.

ROAST MACADAMIA DARK CHOCOLATE BROWNIES

Makes 20

- 100 g macadamias
- 175 g dark chocolate (50% cocoa), broken into pieces
- 125 g unsalted butter
- 75 g (½ cup) plain flour
- ½ teaspoon salt
- ½ teaspoon baking powder
- 3 free-range eggs
- 125 g caster sugar
- 1 teaspoon natural vanilla extract

— Preheat the oven to 140°C (fan-forced). Line a small baking tin with foil. Add the macadamias and roast for 12–15 minutes, shaking the tin every few minutes to ensure they don't burn. Set aside to cool.

— Meanwhile, bring a saucepan of water to the boil. Put the chocolate and butter in a heatproof bowl and set it over the saucepan, ensuring the bottom of the bowl does not touch the water, and stir the mixture regularly until smooth. Remove from the heat and set aside to cool a little.

— Increase the oven temperature to 160°C (fan-forced). Line a 15 cm square baking tin with baking paper.

— Sift the flour, salt and baking powder into a small bowl.

— In a large heatproof bowl, combine the eggs and sugar. Add the melted chocolate and the vanilla extract and whisk vigorously for 1 minute. Gently fold in the flour mixture, a tablespoon at a time, until thoroughly combined. Stir the toasted macadamias through.

— Pour the mixture into the square baking tin and smooth the top with a palette knife. Transfer to the oven and bake for 20 minutes.

— Transfer the baking tin to a wire rack and leave to cool for 10 minutes.

— Remove the brownie from the tin and allow to cool completely before slicing. The brownies will keep in an airtight container for 3–4 days.

BAKED LEMON CHEESECAKE WITH RASPBERRY GLAZE

Serves 8–10

250 g (2 cups) fresh raspberries

BASE

180 g gingernut biscuits

180 g granita biscuits

¼ teaspoon salt

150 g butter, melted

FILLING

250 g (1 cup) sour cream

550 g cream cheese

115 g (½ cup) caster sugar

80 ml (⅓ cup) lemon juice

grated zest of 1 lemon

3 free-range eggs

RASPBERRY GLAZE

250 g frozen raspberries, thawed

1 tablespoon caster sugar

1 teaspoon cornflour

— Preheat the oven to 140°C (fan-forced). Line the base of a 23 cm springform cake tin with baking paper.

— To make the base, blend all the biscuits with the salt in a food processor until the mixture resembles breadcrumbs. Transfer to a bowl and mix in the melted butter. Transfer to the cake tin, pressing down so the crumbs are tightly packed over the base.

— To make the filling, blend the sour cream, cream cheese, sugar, lemon juice and zest in a food processor until well combined, then add the eggs and blend again until just combined.

— Pour the filling over the biscuit base. Leave the mixture to sit for 20 minutes to allow any air bubbles to rise to the surface.

— Gently lift the tin and let it fall on the work surface a few times, to force out any remaining air bubbles.

— Transfer to the oven and bake for 50–60 minutes, or until the filling in the middle of the cheesecake has set, but still wobbles slightly. Turn off the oven, leave the door ajar and leave to cool completely.

— While the cheesecake is in the oven, make the glaze. Purée the raspberries in a blender. Add the puréed raspberries to a small saucepan with the sugar and cornflour, then cook for 4–5 minutes, or until slightly thickened. Set aside to cool.

— Once the cheesecake has cooled, run the edge of a knife around the outer edge of the cheesecake, just to loosen it from the side of the tin. Pour the raspberry glaze over the top, smoothing it out with a knife.

— Transfer to the fridge and leave to cool for 2–3 hours, or overnight.

— When ready to serve, remove from the tin and scatter the fresh raspberries over.

PEACH & BLUEBERRY COBBLER

Serves 6

— Preheat the oven to 160°C (fan-forced). Lightly butter a 1.5 litre (6 cup) baking dish.

— Combine the fruit, sugar, flour, vanilla, spices, orange zest and orange juice in a large bowl. Spoon into the baking dish and set aside.

— To make the topping, combine the flour, hazelnut meal, oats and sugar in a large bowl. Add the butter and use your fingertips to rub the butter into the dry ingredients, until the mixture resembles coarse breadcrumbs.

— In a separate bowl, whisk the egg and milk together. Add to the flour mixture and stir until the dough just comes together — do not over-mix. Spoon heaped tablespoonfuls on top of the fruit mixture, leaving small gaps between the dough.

— Bake for 40–45 minutes, or until the fruit is tender and bubbling, and the topping is well browned and cooked through.

— Dust with icing sugar if you like, and serve with ice cream or cream.

TIP

This recipe also works beautifully with other large stone fruit – try plums or nectarines.

butter, for greasing

800 g peaches, stones removed, cut into wedges

250 g blueberries (fresh or frozen)

80 g (⅓ cup, firmly packed) soft brown sugar

2 tablespoons plain flour

2 teaspoons vanilla bean paste

1 teaspoon ground cinnamon

½ teaspoon freshly grated nutmeg

finely grated zest and juice of 1 orange

sifted icing sugar, for dusting (optional)

ice cream or cream, to serve

TOPPING

150 g (1 cup) self-raising flour, sifted

40 g (⅓ cup) hazelnut meal

30 g (¼ cup) rolled (porridge) oats

2 tablespoons brown sugar

100 g chilled unsalted butter, grated

1 free-range egg, lightly beaten

80 ml (⅓ cup) milk

ROAST BANANA ICE CREAM WITH SALTED CARAMEL PECANS

Makes about 1 litre

500 ml (2 cups) full-cream milk

250 ml (1 cup) cream

30 ml Marsala

2 teaspoons vanilla bean paste

150 g (⅔ cup, firmly packed) brown sugar

5 free-range egg yolks

ROAST BANANAS

2 large ripe bananas, peeled and sliced 1 cm thick

2 tablespoons brown sugar

¼ teaspoon sea salt flakes

SALTED CARAMEL PECANS

55 g (¼ cup) caster sugar

40 g unsalted butter, chopped

1 tablespoon honey

120 g pecans

½ teaspoon sea salt flakes

— Pour the milk, cream and Marsala into a heavy-based saucepan and add the vanilla bean paste.

— Set a large bowl over an ice bath. In another bowl, whisk the sugar and egg yolks until slightly thickened. Whisk the egg yolks into the milk mixture and place the pan over medium heat. Cook, stirring constantly, for about 5 minutes, or until the custard thickens slightly and coats the back of a spoon; it should register 85°C on a cooking thermometer. Strain the custard mixture into the large bowl on the ice bath, discarding any solids, and stir until cold. Cover and refrigerate the custard until well chilled, for at least 2–3 hours, or overnight.

— Preheat the oven to 180°C. Line a baking tray with baking paper. Spread the banana slices on the baking tray and sprinkle with the sugar and salt. Roast for 20–22 minutes, or until lightly caramelised and softened.

— Transfer the bananas to a bowl and roughly mash with a fork. Set aside to cool, then cover and refrigerate until required.

— Line another large baking tray with baking paper. To make the salted caramel pecans, stir the sugar, butter and honey in a small heavy-based saucepan over low heat until the sugar dissolves. Increase the heat to medium and boil, without stirring, for 2–3 minutes, or until the caramel is golden brown. Remove from the heat, add the pecans and swirl the pan to coat them. Working quickly, spread the pecans over the lined baking tray and sprinkle with the salt flakes. Set aside until cool and set, then roughly chop into pieces. (The salted caramel pecans will keep in an airtight container in the pantry for 3–4 days.)

— When the custard is cold, churn it in an ice cream machine according to the manufacturer's instructions. When it begins to thicken (around 15 minutes), add the roast banana and keep churning until very thick. Working quickly, scoop the ice cream into a chilled 1.25 litre (5 cup) container, alternating with a sprinkling of the chopped caramel pecans, reserving some of the pecans to sprinkle over the top.

— Return to the freezer for 2–3 hours, or until firm. Well covered or sealed, the ice cream will keep in the freezer for 3–4 days.

ROAST CHERRY BAKEWELL TART

Serves 10

— To make the pastry, combine the flour and salt in a food processor and blitz briefly. Add the butter and pulse until you have a breadcrumb consistency. Add the egg yolk and pulse a few times to combine. With the motor running, add the water gradually, until the dough forms a ball.

— Wrap in plastic wrap and set aside to rest in the fridge for 1 hour.

— Roll the pastry out between two sheets of baking paper, then use it to line a 20 cm loose-based tart tin. Prick the base with a fork and chill for a further 30 minutes.

— Meanwhile, preheat the oven to 190°C (fan-forced).

— Place the cherries in a baking tin and sprinkle with the orange zest and brown sugar. Toss the mixture until well combined, then bake for about 30 minutes, or until the cherries are soft and caramelised. Set aside to cool.

— Line the rested pastry shell with baking paper, then cover with baking beads, dried beans or rice. Transfer to the oven and blind bake for 10 minutes.

— Remove the baking paper and beads and bake the pastry for a further 10 minutes, or until the base is light brown. Remove from the oven and set aside to cool for 10 minutes.

— Reduce the oven temperature to 160°C (fan-forced).

— Melt the butter in a small saucepan. Transfer to a heatproof bowl and whisk in the sugar and almond meal until well combined. Add the eggs one at a time, whisking lightly after each addition. Finally, fold in the flour.

— Spoon the cherries into the tart shell. Pour the almond mixture over the top and spread evenly with a spatula. Scatter the flaked almonds over the top.

— Bake for 20–25 minutes, or until the almond mixture has risen and a skewer inserted into the middle of the tart comes out clean.

— Serve warm with ice cream.

350 g pitted fresh cherries
grated zest of 1 orange
2 tablespoons soft brown sugar
120 g butter
120 g sugar
120 g (1¼ cups) almond meal
2 free-range eggs
2 tablespoons plain flour
2 tablespoons flaked almonds
ice cream, to serve

PASTRY

150 g (1 cup) plain flour
pinch of salt
60 g cold butter, chopped
1 free-range egg yolk
3–4 tablespoons ice-cold water

INDEX

A
ALMONDS
Almond crumble 154
Roast cherry bakewell tart 173
APPLES
Apple sauce 93
Apple & blueberry pie 157
Chestnut & apple stuffing loaf 66
Roast stuffed pork with apples two ways 86
Sage & apple stuffing 86
Spicy cranberry sauce 79
Asparagus bundles wrapped in prosciutto 126

B
Baby spinach salad 115
BACON
Bacon-wrapped stuffed onions 125
Colcannon 146
Baked lemon cheesecake with raspberry glaze 166
BANANA
Roast banana ice cream 170
Barbecue sauce 107
Barbecued corn salad with chipotle mayo 145
BASIL
New potato salad with fresh herbs & crisp capers 141
Salsa verde 35
BEEF
Beef cheeks in red wine sauce 89
Beef pot roast 108
Boeuf en croute with red wine jus 100
Red wine sauce 89
Roast beef ribs with parsnips & horseradish cream 112
BEETROOT
Roasted root vegies 20
Berbere spice mix 20
BERRIES
Apple & blueberry pie 157
Peach & blueberry cobbler topping 169
Raspberry glaze 166
Roasted berries with almond crumble & rosewater cream 154
Blue cheese sauce 69
Boeuf en croute with red wine jus 100
BREAD
Grissini 158
Brine 92
BROCCOLI
Roasted broccoli salad with pickled onion 149
BROWNIES
Roast macadamia dark chocolate brownies 165
Brussels sprouts with cannellini beans & crumbled pancetta 137
BUTTER
Sage burnt butter 138
Spiced lemon butter 54
BUTTERNUT PUMPKIN
Maple-roasted pumpkin 122

C
CABBAGE
Colcannon 146
Slaw 107
see also red cabbage
Cajun spice mix 47
CANNELLINI BEANS
Brussels sprouts with cannellini beans & crumbled pancetta 137
Lamb shanks with cannellini beans 115
Lemon & rosemary smashed cannellini beans 133
CAPERS
Lemon, herb & caper dressing 149
New potato salad with fresh herbs & crisp capers 141
Salsa verde 35
CAPSICUM
Charred red capsicum sauce 12
Couscous-stuffed capsicum 23
Mediterranean tray bake 142
Peach salsa 111
Slow-roasted rabbit stew 96
CARROTS
Beef pot roast 108
Mediterranean tray bake 142
Orange & thyme roasted baby carrots 150
Roasted root vegies 20
Slaw 107
CASSEROLES AND STEWS
Beef pot roast 108
Lamb shanks with cannellini beans 115
Slow-roasted rabbit stew 96
CAULIFLOWER
Cauliflower & celeriac mash with sage burnt butter 138
Harissa-roasted cauliflower with fig & yoghurt sauce 27
Jalapeño three-cheese cauliflower 129
CELERIAC
Cauliflower & celeriac mash with sage burnt butter 138
Roasted root vegies 20
Charred red capsicum sauce 12
CHEESE
Blue cheese sauce 69
Blue cheese & pine nut stuffing 12
Cheese sauce 129
Jalapeño three-cheese cauliflower 129
Roasted broccoli salad with pickled onion 149
CHEESECAKE
Baked lemon cheesecake with raspberry glaze 166
CHERRIES
Orange & cherry sauce 70
Roast cherry bakewell tart 173
CHESTNUTS
Chestnut & apple stuffing loaf 66
Mushroom & winter vegetable wellington 16
CHICKEN
Chicken in coconut milk 82
Chicken with 40 cloves of garlic & lemon garlic gravy 62
Moroccan-spiced roast chicken with preserved lemon 54
Mushroom-stuffed chicken breasts with garlic cream sauce 58
Roast chicken with walnut & sage stuffing & parsnip gravy 72
Spiced poussin with herbed yoghurt 77
Spicy roasted chicken with blue cheese sauce 69
CHICKPEAS
Roasted root vegies 20
CHILLI
Chicken in coconut milk 82
Chilli ginger dipping sauce 99
Chimichurri 104
Jalapeño three-cheese cauliflower 129
Lime, lemongrass & chilli roasted salmon 43
Mango salsa 47
Peach salsa 111
Romesco sauce 40
Slaw 107
Spiced lemon butter 54
Tomato & chorizo baked fish 39
Chimichurri 104
Chipotle mayo 145
CHIVES
Colcannon 146
New potato salad with fresh herbs & crisp capers 141
Salmon en croute 36
CHOCOLATE
Roast macadamia dark chocolate brownies 165
Roasted white chocolate dip with grissini 158
CHORIZO
Chorizo cranberry stuffing 78
Tomato & chorizo baked fish 39
Cinnamon-roasted peaches with fresh ricotta, thyme & honeyed hazelnuts 162
COBBLER
Peach & blueberry topping 169
Colcannon 146
CORIANDER
Barbecued corn salad with chipotle mayo 145
Herbed yoghurt 77
Mango salsa 47
Peach salsa 111
Spiced lemon butter 54
Whole stuffed pumpkin 24
CORN
Barbecued corn salad with chipotle mayo 145
Couscous-stuffed capsicum 23
CRANBERRIES (DRIED)
Chorizo cranberry stuffing 78
Roasted broccoli salad with pickled onion 149
Spicy cranberry sauce 79
Crispy pork belly with five-spice & dipping sauce 99
Custard for ice cream 170

D
DIP, SWEET
Roasted white chocolate dip with grissini 158
DRESSINGS
Horseradish cream 44, 112
Lemon, herb & caper 149
Salsa verde 35
Dried fig glaze 130
Dry rub 107
DUCK
Roast duck with maple & balsamic glaze 61
Roast duck with orange & cherry sauce 70
Duxelles 100

E
EGGPLANT
Mediterranean tray bake 142
Roasted eggplant with tahini sauce & pomegranate 15

F
FENNEL
Mediterranean tray bake 142
Salmon en papillote 51
FETA
Couscous-stuffed capsicum 23
Roast quail with baked figs, feta & pistachios 65
FIGS
Dried fig glaze 130
Fig & yoghurt sauce 27
Roast figs with vanilla mascarpone 161
Roast quail with baked figs, feta & pistachios 65
FISH
Prosciutto-wrapped fish with Sicilian olives & cherry tomatoes 32

Roast cajun fish 47
testing 'done-ness' 32
Tomato & chorizo baked fish 39
Traditional roast trout with herbs & lemon 44
see also salmon

G

GARLIC
Chicken in coconut milk 82
Chicken with 40 cloves of garlic & lemon garlic gravy 62
Chilli ginger dipping sauce 99
Chimichurri 104
Couscous-stuffed capsicum 23
Duxelles 100
Garlic cream sauce 58
Herbed yoghurt 77
Hoisin & ginger marinade 99
Lemon & rosemary smashed cannellini beans 133
Lemon garlic gravy 62
Lime, lemongrass & chilli roasted salmon 43
Mango salsa 47
Mediterranean tray bake 142
Mushroom & winter vegetable wellington 16
Roast smashed potatoes 134
Roasted garlic & tomato tart 28
Salmon en papillote 51
Salsa verde 35
Spiced poussin with herbed yoghurt 77
Tomato & chorizo baked fish 39
Whole stuffed pumpkin 24

GINGER
Chicken in coconut milk 82
Chilli ginger dipping sauce 99
Hoisin & ginger marinade 99
Lime, lemongrass & chilli roasted salmon 43

GOOSE
Roast goose with chestnut & apple stuffing 66

GRAVY
Lemon garlic gravy 62
Mushroom gravy 17
Parsnip gravy 72

grissini 158

H

HAM
Mustard-glazed roast leg of ham with peach salsa 111

HARISSA 27
Harissa-roasted cauliflower with fig & yoghurt sauce 27

HAZELNUTS
Honeyed hazelnuts 162
Peach & blueberry cobbler topping 169

HERBS
Herb & salt crust 112
Herbed yoghurt 77
Horseradish cream 44, 112
Lemon & herb stuffing 57
Lemon, herb & caper dressing 149
Mediterranean tray bake 142
Salsa verde 35
see also specific herbs

HOISIN SAUCE
Chilli ginger dipping sauce 99
Hoisin & ginger marinade 99

HONEY
Chilli ginger dipping sauce 99
Honeyed hazelnuts 162
Orange & thyme roasted baby carrots 150

Horseradish cream 44, 112

I

ICE CREAM
Roast banana ice cream with salted caramel pecans 170

K

KALE
Mushroom & winter vegetable wellington 16

L

LAMB
Lamb shanks with cannellini beans 115
Mini lamb roasts with chimichurri 104
Slow-roasted Greek lamb with potatoes 90

LEMONS
Baked lemon cheesecake with raspberry glaze 166
Couscous-stuffed capsicum 23
Lemon & herb stuffing 57
Lemon & rosemary smashed cannellini beans 133
Lemon, herb & caper dressing 149
Lemon garlic gravy 62
Lemon-roasted prawns with romesco sauce 40
Mediterranean tray bake 142
Salmon en croute 36
Salmon en papillote 51
Salsa verde 35
Spiced lemon butter 54

LEMONGRASS
Chicken in coconut milk 82
Lime, lemongrass & chilli roasted salmon 43

LIME JUICE AND ZEST
Chicken in coconut milk 82
Chipotle mayo 145
Lime, lemongrass & chilli roasted salmon 43
Mango salsa 47

M

Mango salsa 47

MAPLE SYRUP
Maple & balsamic glaze 61
Maple-roasted pumpkin 122
Mustard-glazed roast leg of ham with peach salsa 111

MASCARPONE
Vanilla mascarpone 161

MAYONNAISE
Chipotle mayo 145
Saffron mayonnaise 48

Mediterranean tray bake 142
Mini lamb roasts with chimichurri 104

MINT
Herbed yoghurt 77
Lemon, herb & caper dressing 149

Moroccan-spiced roast chicken with preserved lemon 54

MUSHROOMS
Duxelles 100
Mushroom & winter vegetable wellington 16
Mushroom gravy 17
Mushroom-stuffed chicken breasts with garlic cream sauce 58
Roast portobello mushrooms with blue cheese & pine nut stuffing 12

MUSTARD
Mustard-glazed roast leg of ham with peach salsa 111
New potato salad with fresh herbs & crisp capers 141
Salmon en croute 36
Salsa verde 35

N

New potato salad with fresh herbs & crisp capers 141

NUTS
Roast macadamia dark chocolate brownies 165
Roast quail with baked figs, feta & pistachios 65
Roasted root vegies 20
see also almonds; hazelnuts; pecans; walnuts

O

OLIVES
Mediterranean tray bake 142
Prosciutto-wrapped fish with Sicilian olives & cherry tomatoes 32
Slow-roasted rabbit stew 96

ONIONS
Baby spinach salad 115
Bacon-wrapped stuffed onions 125
Beef pot roast 108
Mediterranean tray bake 142
Peach salsa 111
Quick pickled onions 149

ORANGE JUICE AND ZEST
Chestnut & apple stuffing loaf 66
Orange & cherry sauce 70
Orange & thyme roasted baby carrots 150
Peach & blueberry cobbler topping 169
Roast cherry bakewell tart 173

OREGANO
Cajun spice mix 47
Chimichurri 104

P

PANCETTA
Brussels sprouts with cannellini beans & crumbled pancetta 137
Slow-roasted rabbit stew 96

PAPRIKA
Barbecue sauce 107
Cajun spice mix 47
Spiced lemon butter 54
Spicy roasted chicken with blue cheese sauce 69
Tomato & chorizo baked fish 39

PARSLEY
Chestnut & apple stuffing loaf 66
Chimichurri 104
Couscous-stuffed capsicum 23
Herb & salt crust 112
Herbed yoghurt 77
Lemon, herb & caper dressing 149
New potato salad with fresh herbs & crisp capers 141
Romesco sauce 40
Walnut & sage stuffing 73

PARSNIPS
Parsnip gravy 72
Roast beef ribs with parsnips & horseradish cream 112
Roasted root vegies 20

PASTRIES, SAVOURY
Boeuf en croute with red wine jus 100
Mushroom & winter vegetable wellington 16
Roasted garlic & tomato tart 28
Salmon en croute 36

PASTRY
lattice top 157
sweet pie 157
tarts 28, 173

PEACHES
Cinnamon-roasted peaches with fresh ricotta, thyme & honeyed hazelnuts 162
Peach & blueberry cobbler topping 169
Peach salsa 111

PECANS
caramelising 122
Chorizo cranberry stuffing 78
Maple-roasted pumpkin 122
Salted caramel pecans 170

PICKLED ONIONS
Quick pickled onion 149

PIES, SWEET
Apple & blueberry pie 157
lattice pastry top 157

PINE NUTS
Roast portobello mushrooms with blue cheese & pine nut stuffing 12

POMEGRANATE
Roasted eggplant with tahini sauce & pomegranate 15

POMEGRANATE MOLASSES
Roast quail with baked figs, feta & pistachios 65

PORK
crackling 86, 99
Crispy pork belly with five-spice & dipping sauce 99

PORK, *CONTINUED*
Pork knuckle with apple sauce & sauerkraut 92
resting 93, 99
Roast stuffed pork with apples two ways 86
Sage & apple stuffing 86
Sticky roast pork ribs with slaw 107
PORK SAUSAGES
Chestnut & apple stuffing loaf 66
Lemon & herb stuffing 57
POTATOES
Beef pot roast 108
Colcannon 146
New potato salad with fresh herbs & crisp capers 141
Roast smashed potatoes 134
Salmon en papillote 51
Slow-roasted Greek lamb with potatoes 90
Thyme & sumac hasselback potatoes 118
PRAWNS
Lemon-roasted prawns with romesco sauce 40
PRESERVED LEMON
Moroccan-spiced roast chicken with preserved lemon 54
Spiced lemon butter 54
PROSCIUTTO
Asparagus bundles wrapped in prosciutto 126
Boeuf en croute with red wine jus 100
Prosciutto-wrapped fish with Sicilian olives & cherry tomatoes 32
PUMPKIN
Roasted root vegies 20
Whole stuffed pumpkin 24
see also butternut pumpkin

Q
QUAIL
Roast quail with baked figs, feta & pistachios 65
Quick pickled onion 149

R
RABBIT
Slow-roasted rabbit stew 96
Raspberry glaze 166
RED CABBAGE
Roasted red cabbage with dried fig glaze 130
Red wine jus 101
Red wine sauce 89
RICOTTA
Cinnamon-roasted peaches with fresh ricotta, thyme & honeyed hazelnuts 162
Mediterranean tray bake 142
Roasted garlic & tomato tart 28
Roast banana ice cream with salted caramel pecans 170
Roast beef ribs with parsnips & horseradish cream 112
Roast cajun fish 47
Roast cherry bakewell tart 173
Roast chicken with walnut & sage stuffing & parsnip gravy 72
Roast duck with maple & balsamic glaze 61
Roast duck with orange & cherry sauce 70
Roast figs with vanilla mascarpone 161
Roast goose with chestnut & apple stuffing 66
Roast macadamia dark chocolate brownies 165
Roast portobello mushrooms with blue cheese & pine nut stuffing 12
Roast quail with baked figs, feta & pistachios 65
Roast smashed potatoes 134
Roast stuffed pork with apples two ways 86
Roast turkey with spicy cranberry sauce 78
Roasted berries with almond crumble & rosewater cream 154
Roasted broccoli salad with pickled onion 149
Roasted eggplant with tahini sauce & pomegranate 15
Roasted garlic & tomato tart 28
Roasted red cabbage with dried fig glaze 130
Roasted root vegies 20
Roasted shellfish platter 48
Roasted white chocolate dip with grissini 158
Rolled turkey breast with lemon & herb stuffing 57
Romesco sauce 40
ROSEMARY
Herb & salt crust 112
Lemon & rosemary smashed cannellini beans 133
Mediterranean tray bake 142
Roast smashed potatoes 134
Thyme & sumac hasselback potatoes 118

S
Saffron mayonnaise 48
SAGE
Bacon-wrapped stuffed onions 125
Chestnut & apple stuffing loaf 66
Roasted eggplant with tahini sauce & pomegranate 15
Sage & apple stuffing 86
Sage burnt butter 138
Walnut & sage stuffing 73
SALADS
Baby spinach salad 115
Barbecued corn salad with chipotle mayo 145
New potato salad with fresh herbs & crisp capers 141
Roasted broccoli salad with pickled onion 149
SALMON
Lime, lemongrass & chilli roasted salmon 43
Salmon en croute 36
Salmon en papillote 51
SALSA
Mango salsa 47
Peach salsa 111
Salsa verde 35
SAUCES
Apple 93
Barbecue 107
Blue cheese 69
Charred red capsicum 12
Cheese 129
Chilli ginger dipping 99
Fig & yoghurt 27
Garlic cream 58
Orange & cherry 70
Red wine 89
Romesco 40
Spicy cranberry 79
Tahini 15, 20
SHELLFISH
Roasted shellfish platter 48
SHERRY
Orange & cherry sauce 70
Roast figs with vanilla mascarpone 161
Roasted red cabbage with dried fig glaze 130
Slaw 107
Slow-roasted Greek lamb with potatoes 90
Slow-roasted rabbit stew 96
Snapper in a salt crust 35
SPICES
Berbere spice mix 20
Cajun spice mix 47
Cinnamon-roasted peaches with fresh ricotta, thyme & honeyed hazelnuts 162
Couscous-stuffed capsicum 23
Crispy pork belly with five-spice & dipping sauce 99
Moroccan-spiced roast chicken with preserved lemon 54
Peach & blueberry cobbler 169
Spiced lemon butter 54
Spiced poussin with herbed yoghurt 77
Spicy cranberry sauce 79
Spicy roasted chicken with blue cheese sauce 69
Tahini sauce 15, 20
SPINACH
Baby spinach salad 115
Salmon en croute 36
STEWS
Slow-roasted rabbit stew 96
Sticky roast pork ribs with slaw 107
STUFFINGS
Blue cheese & pine nut 12
Chestnut & apple 66
Chorizo cranberry 78
Lemon & herb 57
Sage & apple 86
Walnut & sage 73
SUMAC
Roasted root vegies 20
Spiced lemon butter 54
Thyme & sumac hasselback potatoes 118

T
Tahini sauce 15, 20
TARTS
pastry 28, 173
Roast cherry bakewell tart 173
Roasted garlic & tomato tart 28
THYME
Bacon-wrapped stuffed onions 125
Duxelles 100
Mediterranean tray bake 142
Mushroom & winter vegetable wellington 16
Orange & thyme roasted baby carrots 150
Red wine jus 101
Thyme & sumac hasselback potatoes 118
TOMATOES
Barbecue sauce 107
Lamb shanks with cannellini beans 115
Mediterranean tray bake 142
Mini lamb roasts with chimichurri 104
Peach salsa 111
Prosciutto-wrapped fish with Sicilian olives & cherry tomatoes 32
Roasted garlic & tomato tart 28
Romesco sauce 40
Slow-roasted rabbit stew 96
Tomato & chorizo baked fish 39
Traditional roast trout with herbs &lemon 44
TURKEY
Chorizo cranberry stuffing 78
cooking time 57, 79
resting 79
Rolled turkey breast with lemon & herb stuffing 57
Roast turkey with spicy cranberry sauce 78

V
Vanilla mascarpone 161

W
Walnut & sage stuffing 73
Whole stuffed pumpkin 24
WINE
Beef pot roast 108
Boeuf en croute with red wine jus 100
Duxelles 100
Garlic cream sauce 58
Red wine jus 101
Red wine sauce 89
Salmon en papillote 51
Slow-roasted Greek lamb with potatoes 90
Slow-roasted rabbit stew 96
see also sherry

Y
YOGHURT
Fig & yoghurt sauce 27
Herbed yoghurt 77
Tahini sauce 15, 20
Yorkshire puddings 121

Z
ZUCCHINI
Mediterranean tray bake 142